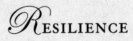

RESILIENCE

Also by Elizabeth Edwards

SAVING GRACES

ELIZABETH EDWARDS

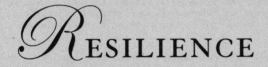RESILIENCE

Reflections on the Burdens and Gifts
of Facing Life's Adversities

BROADWAY BOOKS
New York

BROADWAY

Copyright © 2009, 2010 by Elizabeth Edwards

All rights reserved.
Published in the United States by Broadway Books,
an imprint of the Crown Publishing Group,
a division of Random House, Inc., New York.
www.crownpublishing.com

BROADWAY BOOKS and the Broadway Books colophon are
trademarks of Random House, Inc.

Originally published in hardcover in slightly different form in the
United States by Broadway Books, an imprint of the Crown Publishing
Group, a division of Random House, Inc., New York, in 2009.

"The Red Dress," from *The Portable Dorothy Parker*
by Dorothy Parker, edited by Marion Meade, copyright © 1928, renewed
1956 by Dorothy Parker. Used by permission of Viking Penguin,
a division of Penguin Group (USA) Inc.

Library of Congress Cataloging-in-Publication Data
Edwards, Elizabeth, 1949–
Resilience : reflections on the burdens and gifts of facing
life's adversities / Elizabeth Edwards.—1st ed.
p. cm.
1. Edwards, Elizabeth, 1949– 2. Edwards, Elizabeth, 1949– —
Philosophy. 3. Resilience (Personality trait) 4. Legislators' spouses—
United States—Biography. 5. Cancer—Patients—United
States—Biography. 6. Lawyers' spouses—North Carolina—Biography.
7. Edwards, John, 1953 June 10– 8. Edwards, John, 1953 June 10– —
Family. 9. North Carolina—Biography. I. Title.
E840.8.E29E23 2009
973.931092—dc22
[B]
2009009061

ISBN 978-0-7679-3156-4

PRINTED IN THE UNITED STATES OF AMERICA

Design by Tina Henderson

1 3 5 7 9 10 8 6 4 2

First Paperback Edition

To my parents,
Vince and Elizabeth Anania

ACKNOWLEDGMENTS

The act of looking forward after a setback is a solitary act, as is writing. But it would be wrong to suggest that no one else played a role. In my case, the looking forward was possible—no, necessary—because of my children, Cate, Emma Claire, and Jack and the memory of Wade. I acknowledge not only their importance in writing this book but in allowing me the gift of looking forward in life. It is a gift, but also a learned skill, and I learned it from my parents, Vince and Liz Anania, to whom I dedicate this book.

In the writing, I was encouraged and supported by my family, my brother Jay Anania and my sister Nancy Anania, and by my dear friend Glenn Bergenfield.

It may seem obligatory to thank one's editor, but in this case it is accurate. Stacy Creamer was with me through a very difficult time and was supportive of every decision I made about writing, not writing, writing. I cannot imagine a finer, more understanding editor.

Resilience

CHAPTER I

1990

I stood at the sink in an impossibly bright hospital room washing my face, washing away the heat that, with the doctor's words, had come rushing to my face and neck and chest to fill every pore, to gather in the corners of my eyes and to line my lips and thicken my tongue. "He will never walk, his brain is dead," the doctor had said. It still burned. How much cold water would it take to take the hot sting out of those words?

My father lay immobile behind me, a crisp sheet folded neatly across his chest, the crease apparently to be forever perfect above his forever-still form. I had not been able to bear to see him like that any longer, so I had turned away and instead watched my own warped reflection in the metal mirror that seemed to mimic the distortions within me. The doctor's words were all I could hear inside my head, but they were too immense, too life-changing to stay in my head. They spilled out and filled the room, bouncing back from the walls and the metal me in the mirror, and with every echo a new torment: *He will not walk. His brain is dead. He will not walk. His brain is dead.* . . . I kept cupping water to my face, unable to cool the heat but equally unable to stop trying.

The day before, this solid man who would be seventy in four days, who still had cannonballs for shoulders and the calf muscles of a twenty-five-year-old fullback, had fallen over while eating a salad for dinner. He had played tennis in the morning and had gone biking in the afternoon. He came in to dinner after planting spring flowers in the yard. Every minute of his day was a test of his body, a test he passed over and over again. And then, with no warning, a massive stroke, and he could not move from the floor. I was forty years old, and I had never seen him fail at a single physical thing he had tried to do. Not once in forty years.

I closed my eyes as I cupped the water, and the images of my well father, strong and full of life, gathered on top of one another. Eating a hot pepper from his garden in Naples and thinking it a green pepper, his face goes flush, tears fill his eyes, his glasses fog up, but he chews on. And then, grinning at his astonished family, he gets up and picks another. The awestruck faces of the enlisted men he commanded in Japan when he came out of the pool into which they had thrown him and, with his soaking wet flight suit clinging to him, they saw his supremely muscled form outlined. News that he had made captain had come in while he was on an early-morning flight, so when he stepped out of the jet in his flight suit, his squadron had rallied around him cheering and had thrown him into the pool in giddy celebration. I always suspected that the vision of him earned him a respect from those enlisted men that morning that the additional stripe on his sleeve would not have won him.

I had sat with him at Bethesda Naval Hospital when he had four discs in his spine fused, the final remedy two decades after his back was injured when the wheels on the jet he was getting ready to pilot collapsed beneath the plane on the tarmac. He should have been groggy and still in the hours after recovery, but he was smiling at everyone, and teasing the nurses by pretending to smoke an endless series of imaginary cigarettes. Within weeks, he was back on his bicycle, and within months, he was back on the tennis court. There was the time his nose was flattened in college in a football game. The doctors said it was so crushed that he could choose whatever shape he wanted since they were starting from scratch. So he chose the shape he had had before. And he took up lacrosse, and he was an all-American his first year. He used to lift women up—my mother and her friends—and twirl them head over heels like batons. Proper women in 1950s shirtwaists ignored the fact that their garter belts had been on display, and they giggled to be treated as girls again. He carried my brother, my sister, and me all at once on his wide shoulders upstairs to bed when we were youngsters as if we were stuffed animals. Now, impossibly, he lay dying behind me, unable to move, unable to speak.

The doctor had called us into the room to tell us. My sister sat with her arm around my mother. My brother sat holding our father's hand. I stood at the foot of the bed, my eyes on my father's still face, not on the doctor I had never seen before. Each of us cried, not in a wailing way, but in low, lonely moans. The doctor talked on about the effect of the stroke on the blood flow to his brain, and we each half-listened, for truthfully nothing after "his brain

4

is dead" could penetrate. Tracks of silent tears covered all of our cheeks. When the doctor left, we all hugged one another, grieving our collective loss and our individual ones, then everyone else left the room. I had to tell my children, ten-year-old Wade and eight-year-old Cate, where they waited in the hall with their father. And I had to wash my face before I would tell them.

I could clean the tear tracks, but the heat would not go away. I gave up and turned to leave and face the children. As I turned, I looked again at my father, but now he was looking back. He was still immobile, his huge bulk still pinned beneath the tight sheets, but his eyes were open. Not just open but wide dishes of panic. He could not speak. And yet he did. We stood staring at one another—I haven't any idea how long—and he said, or his eyes said, *I am here. I am not dead. I am here. I want to live.* I answered back in words. "Don't worry," I said. "We know. We are not giving up on you." And I marched past my family to the nurses' station and told them that that doctor was not allowed back into my father's room under any circumstances.

This was April 18, 1990. We buried my father in April of 2008. Oh, his body kept failing him, little by little until the last of him slipped away eighteen years later. But in between he learned to drive again (in a fairly frightening fashion), and drove until his response time was demonstrably too slow and we could not let him drive any longer. He talked again, in an odd and sometimes inappropriately scatalogical way—"the boobs are boiling"—but still making people smile, until he no longer could talk easily, and losing confidence in his voice, he started talking again with his eyes. He danced with my mother for nearly a dozen more years. He never biked or played tennis again, but he traveled. He went to Poland and Spain, he took a cruise and watched the whales off the Alaskan coast. He voted for his son-in-law for vice president of the United States. And he was there to bury his oldest grandson—my first-born. But he was also there to hold four more grandchildren—Ty and Louis and Emma Claire and Jack—and even two great-grandchildren—Anna and Zachary—who were born after his stroke. In the end, he was surrounded by family—his wife of nearly sixty years, his children and grandchildren, his sister and her children—when finally, of his own will, he quit fighting and let go.

There were times in the eighteen years more

that he lived when he wanted to give up, when he didn't want to keep fighting to drive or to dance or to live. I remember sitting with him once after my son Wade died. We were going through a workbook his rehabilitation therapist had assigned him. I would read; he would answer questions. He got them right at first, and then he started to miss them, a few at first and then all of them. His frustration mounted, and he finally said with awkward resignation that he was a burden he promised himself he would never be and he would just as soon die. I was stunned and angry. I wanted him to live so badly; how could he not want it, too? If you could have Wade back, I asked, but only in your exact condition, no better, would you take him? He raised his head a little, and his deep brown eyes met mine. He nodded. Then you understand how we feel. We know it is not perfect, but nothing really ever is. I reached for his hand and told him you are here, and that is what I want. And, I added, if you think this is getting you out of finishing this assignment, you are wrong. He opened his mouth. It was not the wide smile I remembered, but the gap between his two front teeth showed, and that was smile enough for me.

There is nothing about resilience that I can say that my father did not first utter silently in eighteen years of living inside a two-dimensional cutout of himself. From the first moment when he forced open his eyes to tell me that he was alive, through all the setbacks of a body on which he had relied that subsequently failed him little by little, he held on to whatever he had, however meager it was. He managed somehow to turn whatever he held on to into precisely what he needed to survive. When in the first year he had the audacity to tell the rehabilitation counselor that he wanted to drive, or when in the eighth year he danced with my mother, or when in year sixteen he unabashedly flirted with the aide at the assisted-living center, he was saying to the world what he said to me in 1990: I understand that it will not be all I crave, but I want to live. And so he did. When he could no longer drive himself, he wanted to walk. When he could no longer walk himself, he wanted a wheelchair that he could manage himself. He kept narrowing his life and his expectations to what he had left, and in doing so—no matter how small his world—he always reflected the sheer majesty of living.

Too many times I have had to use my father's strength—or my mother's grace as she stood beside him—as a touchstone. I suspect we each have someone like him, someone whose personal courage in the face of impossible odds inspires us to do something we thought we could not do, who reminds us that what seems like a mountain in front of us can in fact be climbed. My father was an imperfect man in many ways, but maybe it was better that he was imperfect and that I knew he was, for I learned that perfection was not a requirement of resilience. This was Dad, and if he could decide to live, so could I.

CHAPTER 2

Introduction

𝒯he culture of celebrity informs our lives in such a way that we seem to know much too much about someone's life until—pop!—we know nothing at all. Ultimately interest wanes, and the media's laser focus moves on to other subject-targets. It was not so long ago that Lee Atwater changed politics in America, and some—as I—would say not in a positive way. But ask his name on the street and you may not find a single person who knows it. A friend of mine asked his college class how many knew something about Brigitte Bardot, and they had never heard of her at all. Some celebrities remain familiar through the decades. The appetite for tales about John F. Kennedy, for example, never seems sated. And yet do we really understand who he was?

Judas Iscariot has remained infamous through the centuries for his betrayal of Jesus. Yet I am betting there is another biblical character, someone once almost as notorious as Judas, who is now much less widely known. Just as the words *traitor* and *Judas* became synonymous, there was a time when *Ananias* and *liar* were near synonyms, too. In the Acts of the Apostles, Ananias lied to Jesus about his money so he would not have to give as much to the church. The story was once so renowned that, not so long ago, when someone wanted to brand President Theodore Roosevelt as a liar, he simply said he was a member of the Ananias Club.

Few today, except those who fill in Will Shortz's crossword puzzles, would know that *Ananias* is still a common clue for the four-letter entry *liar*. (Since my maiden name is Anania, I do not consider this an entirely unfortunate lapse in our national attention span. My father appeared before the House Armed Services Committee in 1958, and South Carolina congressman Mendel Rivers asked him, since his last name was Anania, if his word was to be trusted.) But the ebb and flow of celebrity constantly remind me that whatever fortunes and calamities have blessed or befallen me, and however they have given me some notoriety, that notoriety will be—if I am lucky—fleeting.

For those who know me well, I suppose you can

skip forward, but for the rest of you, I am Elizabeth and I have lived an extraordinary life in nearly every sense of the word.

I was born in 1949, the daughter of a Navy pilot and his wife, who was also the daughter of a Navy pilot. My brother and my sister were born in 1950 and 1951, and the troop of us crossed the globe a half-dozen times following my father so he could fly and spy and fight in wars. I watched my friends bury their pilot fathers; I came perilously close to burying my own father; I watched some of my friends march off to wars in which they would die. I grew up largely without American television or the emergence of the shopping mall, and I listened, on Armed Forces Radio, more to Rosemary Clooney and Jeri Southern than to Ricky Nelson and Elvis Presley, all because I spent most of my growing-up years in Japan.

Maybe it is because I remember those days with Nat King Cole in the background as so idyllic that I had a notion that a magical life was built around music that sounded like Armed Forces Radio. At ten, I could paint a fantasy life—and I did—based on the music to which I listened and on the books I read. And at sixteen, I did the same thing. The books changed, but the music did not. My internal world was set to song.

I lived beside a war, the Vietnam War, but even then I romanticized the soldiers, their girls back home, and I had the music of World War I and World War II from which to choose. I lived in Japan at the time and Armed Forces Radio didn't play any antiwar songs. On my radio it was "I'll Be Seeing You" and "The White Cliffs of Dover" and "It's Been a Long, Long Time." They all turned out the same: *Never thought that you would be standing here so close to me. There's so many things that I should say, but words can wait until some other day. Just kiss me once, then kiss me twice, then kiss me once again. It's been a long, long time.*

And I thought I was living that magical life when I went to college at the end of an era when young men in suits picked up their dates at the train station and carried their suitcase to an approved house of a matronly hostess in charge, presumably, of the girl's chastity for the weekend, where witty men and clever women sat in smoky jazz bars and talked only of important things, where no one washed dishes alone or ate alone, where people sang around a piano at Christmas. I was living a life I had heard and read of, with Benny Goodman in the background, where handsome men caressed pretty women with a passion that must be reserved for those who did not know if they would ever kiss again. The fact that it never was a reality did not mean it wasn't my chosen reality. I wanted that old-fashioned world of private passion and unadorned beauty and a life constructed around things of purity and purpose. I wanted it in college and in law school and for most of my growing-up years. I hadn't grown up in a world in which these romantic images were corrupted in any way. Until they were. Even when I had to accept that the soldiers were not coming home to pigtailed sweethearts on country lanes, that the color of your skin gave you a whole different, less hospitable country, that there was real hardship and pain everywhere, I still wanted to escape to that fantasy when I could. My expectations for life were based on that fantasy.

When I was faced with a less pleasant reality, as when I read Truman Capote's *In Cold Blood* at sixteen, I simply concluded it was an aberration, the ugliness of criminal minds imposed on the beauty of the idyllic home. John Updike's people, falling apart from lack of character, were a curiosity. My people belonged to Henry James, and they fell away from joy or grace because of the splendor of their characters. I thought in song. When I couldn't think in song, I could pull out the lyrics book I had been constructing since college. First a hundred songs, then a thousand, now five thousand, and there I could find the soundtrack I preferred for my life. In song, as in Henry James's novels, faults all turned out to be virtues, as if written by Sammy Cahn: *I'm irresponsibly mad for you.* I had, I have to say, a long, long way to fall when the fall finally came.

I married my law school sweetheart, John, on a hot summer day in North Carolina, and we walked through life in a carefree way. We really did have the two children, a picturesque two-story white frame house, the golden retriever, and the station wagon. My husband made a name for himself as a lawyer; I slipped back into a hybrid life of being the lawyer I was supposed to be and the mother I needed to be. When things were not right, well, we just fixed them, in our lives, in the lives of others. Sometimes money could fix a problem; sometimes it was simply a matter of being wise enough to know which string to pull. But we always fixed what needed to be fixed and our ride together had its own music. Our house became the place where life happened; there were young people gathered in the kitchen; there was a basketball game on the cement court behind the house. It seemed that whatever we had done, we had done right.

It would have been easy for life to have played itself out from that kitchen, and I don't know that, if it had, it would have occurred to me that I had never taken in the fullest breath I could. It had been diaphragmatic breathing, matching my inhaling and exhaling to some rhythm I wanted, some song that fit my life at the time, or I thought did. I had never had to find my own rhythm, never needed to search for my own cadence. If the music's cadence was drowned out, it was usually by John's or the children's, and I walked to that. When I needed my own, I would fall back into Jerome Kern. For all of the times that followed those carefree days in my kitchen, for all of the pain I endured, at least I learned in the years that followed what it meant to breathe for myself, and I learned, too, what it meant to scream.

Wade, my firstborn, died on April 4, 1996. An April wind crossed the tobacco fields of eastern North Carolina and pushed the car of which he was so very proud from the road. He was sixteen, and maybe it would not have mattered how old he was, but he did not know how to get it back on the road without flipping it. So it flipped. And flipped, and flipped, until all of the life of the boy was pressed from him. And from me.

I move on now, but I will be back. I always come back to Wade. But I cannot tell the rest of the story if I let myself fall into him now.

Our surviving family held together, or rather we were held together by an extraordinary fourteen-year-old girl, our daughter Cate, who managed to be what we needed and to allow us to look for new paths, paths that she knew would further upset her life, but she kept saying yes. Yes, go back to work, Dad. Yes, try to have another child. Yes, run for the U.S. Senate if that is what you want. It wasn't perfect; she was a teenage girl who had been feeling her budding wings. But given the loss of Wade, she knew it wasn't the time, so she placed her own dreams in a box and put them away for a time.

So we had that one new child, Emma Claire, and then another, Jack, and John did win the Senate seat, so soon it was sounds other than those of teenage boys in our Raleigh kitchen. Life was changing quickly. Wade died in 1996. John won the Senate seat in 1998, the year Emma Claire was born. Cate graduated from high school three weeks after Jack was born in 2000. By the fall of 2000, that kitchen in Raleigh was empty. Cate was off to college and to a life blessedly away from all the pain that had been—and from the turmoil that was to come. The remaining four of us were in a spacious home in Washington. Since I had lived a life of being up-rooted, I should have been used to it enough to move to Washington without a look back. But this time I was leaving the house in which I had expected to die, and I was leaving Wade's grave to live 250 miles away. And it wasn't so often our kitchen in Raleigh anymore in which we gathered but a more empty kitchen in Washington. We slept in the Raleigh house less and less often, and sometimes saw our dear friends back there only at Christmas. I had to make special trips to change the plantings at Wade's grave. It took me some time to get my bearings.

The younger children, the picture of resilience, grew and thrived in a series of homes in Washing-ton, D.C., and then, when my husband decided to run for the nomination for president and then as the nominee for vice president, in a series of hotel rooms and in the homes of generous strangers.

And except for missing Wade and regretting what he had lost, life had a good cadence again, an odd public cadence but a rhythm we all learned.

If you really did not know me then, you would need to know only that I was moderately well-liked by the press for being unscripted (and unscriptable, if that can be bastardized into a word) and candid. I was reasonably well-liked by the Democrats for being well-informed and accessible, an actual mother and not a mother figure. I was even a favorite of opposing extremists because I was chubby enough to be made fun of and unschooled enough politically to say something now and again that they could take out of context and use as fodder. Then the election of 2004 ended, the Democrats, John Kerry and my husband, who should have won given all the issues, in fact lost, and on the very next day I confirmed a diagnosis I had suspected in the weeks before the election: I had breast cancer. Even the opposition laid down their arms.

The treatment was not easy, but, honestly, after Wade's death, I could do it. There were days when it was hard, but I could fight and that was all I needed. It is what I hadn't had with Wade: a chance to fight. I remember telling my father, his right hand clinched perpetually half-open, that if Wade was alive he would fight. I told myself the same thing, and everything after that was easier. John sat with me in chemotherapies, often reading as I slept or calling people to thank them for their help in the election. And he would bring me dinner in bed when I didn't want to climb the steps of our four-story Washington house again. And by the end of my treatments we had moved back to North Carolina, first to the house that had been Wade's home, and then to a rental house in Chapel Hill from which we watched our new home being built. Finally, we moved into that new family home on an old tobacco farm outside Chapel Hill, idyllic and peaceful with promises of a long life as an old couple with children who were still impossibly young.

That was the story from my side. John thought still about running for president again. He traveled, giving speeches, talking of poverty, about which he and I care deeply, raising money for efforts to increase the minimum wage and start antipoverty programs. I stayed home and wrote a book about the journey on which we had found ourselves over the previous decade. The children started public school. And, without my knowing, a woman who spotted my husband one afternoon in the restaurant bar of the hotel in which he was staying hung around outside the hotel for a couple of hours until he returned from a dinner and introduced herself by saying, "You are so hot."

There is a Dorothy Parker poem of which I am fond that captures the flow of my life.

The Red Dress
I always saw, I always said
If I were grown and free,
I'd have a gown of reddest red
As fine as you could see,
To wear out walking, sleek and slow,
Upon a Summer day,
And there'd be one to see me so
And flip the world away.
And he would be a gallant one,
With stars behind his eyes,
And hair like metal in the sun,
And lips too warm for lies.
I always saw us, gay and good,
High honored in the town.
Now I am grown to womanhood. . . .
I have the silly gown.

CHAPTER 3

1965

*M*y father was wearing his greens, a foresty olive uniform with a sewn-down belt on the jacket. Like the music I loved, it was a throwback. In the Navy, only aviators wore the uniform. I loved the feel of it, and because it didn't wrinkle or stain like his dress whites, I could hug him hard and feel him. And this day, an early-fall day in 1965, I needed to touch him. I was sixteen years old and he was going to Vietnam. On the day he was to leave, he stood near the end of the low bleachers on the visitors' side of the Chofu High School football field, watching me cheer in my first game as a cheerleader.

And then his duffel bags were in the car, where my mother, my brother, and my sister waited for him. He would say good-bye to me at halftime, and they would drive him to Tachikawa Air Base, and he would fly to Tan Son Nhut Air Base in Vietnam. The rest of us would go home to our house at Camp

Zama, Japan, and wait until his tour of duty was over or until he was injured or until a chaplain knocked on our door and told us he had been killed. Then we could go back to the States, with him or without him. I was lucky; a year later, we went home with him.

He had been to war before—once, in World War II before he and my mother met, and again, in Korea when I was a youngster. I was in elementary school when he was a reconnaissance pilot during the Cold War, when his plane was shot at, likely by North Korean MiG fighter planes in a conflict a bit unreal for a nine-year-old. War was what the base children played to fill a summer—boys against girls—and the Cold War cost some of those children their parents, but as real as the images are to me even today of the memorial services for lost pilots and crews, the real costs of that war were an abstraction.

But the Vietnam War wasn't an abstraction to me. We had no television in Japan, where Dad was stationed before Vietnam, but the ways we did get news—the *Stars and Stripes* military newspaper and Armed Forces Radio—were blanketed in this war. No detail was too small for the most interested of audiences. The base on which we lived was the home base for a military hospital nearby to which the Army first brought wounded soldiers from Vietnam, and we would see them at the hospital and, sometimes as they readied to return to war, on base. A quiet, handsome young man, not much older than I, maneuvering in a wheelchair, his one remaining leg in a cast. The war. The bandaged fellow walking with him, with features too large for his face and raw meaty scars across his neck, who never stopped talking. The war. The boy across the table who looked a little like my lab partner in chemistry but who could not look you in the eye. Rows of beds, and a seemingly endless line of casualties, most of whom looked like my brother, my friends.

We would see the wounded, at the Depot, the hospital at Sagami-Ono where the most physically able would sit with a teenage volunteer, or in my case a teenage cheerleader, intended to be a moment of normalcy in a life turned upside down. They might have talked to some of my classmates about what happened to them in the war, what they saw, but when I would see them across the table at the hospital, they all talked about the same thing: going home. Even if they knew they would be headed back to combat, all they wanted to talk about was home. And the home they talked about was the home they left—left when they had two legs, left without shrapnel scars across their chest and neck, left before the images of war that would scar the places where the doctors couldn't reach. That's the home they craved. The one before.

Men like my father have been going off to war for all of recorded time. And all of them have come back from war changed some, and some have come back almost different men. In the wars of early civilization it was called a trembling; later it was shell shock, then battle fatigue; finally, in the 1970s, we gave it a medical name—post-traumatic stress disorder. All were a form of war neuroses, but whatever the name, many of those men who went to war as courageous soldiers came home with the war still inside them. Courageous or cowardly, strong or weak, there was no predicting it. A solder blinded at the Battle of Marathon when he witnessed the warrior to his side struck dead. An infantryman who developed a facial tic after stabbing an enemy soldier in the face with a bayonet. Physical manifestations of a psychological wound. A Vietnam veteran awaking in a sweat with a half-remembered horror played out in the darkness. And it is repeated

war after war. The Greatest Generation from World
War II was not simply too humble to take credit for
their accomplishments in battle (though they were
often that), they were also good men too stunned
that what they had seen was now part of their own
life story. The son of a dairyman being asked to shoot
young German boys, his own age, as they emerged
wounded from a foxhole. They watched men with
whom they had eaten dinner the night before be
blown into unidentifiable pieces. Maybe if they never
said it out loud, it would not be so. But it was so, and
too many died years after the war with their stories
silently eating at them from the inside. *Life* magazine described Tom Lea's painting of a tormented
World War II marine as "the two thousand yard
stare," looking out at nothing at all, unable to focus
on the world that was close enough to touch.

Some from Vietnam tried to quiet the war
within with drugs or alcohol. They had left for war
as young men who made Mother's Day cards and
helped their grandfathers bring in firewood, who
tried three times to call that girl in their biology
class before getting the courage even to say hello.
They had served because they were called or because they felt a duty or because they had nowhere

else to go. They left as young men and came back as old men. They were, as are all soldiers from chess boards to desert battlefields, actors in a play gone awry, when all the ways in which we avoid unspeakable inhumanity to one another have failed. Only, it wasn't just knocking over someone's knight. It wasn't figurative at all. They witnessed and lived the worst horrors that man can perpetrate on man. It must be impossible to go back to the spirit of the boy making that Mother's Day card. And some did not, and the mothers and wives and brothers and fathers recognized only the physical man who returned from war.

Ajax went off to the Trojan War and came back a still man, half-empty. Near the end of this terrible war, Ajax expected an honor befitting his heroics, but the honor went elsewhere, and Ajax went mad. Perhaps the honor, had it come, might have forestalled the madness; perhaps nothing would have warded it off. But Ajax's madness played out as he committed atrocities against animals as if they were human enemies. His story is tragic, but the universality of it is made very clear by Tecmessa, the wife to whom he returns in Sophocles' play. He is forever changed by war and by his recognition of what he is capable of doing. She begs for help for him. "He used to grieve but never wail aloud—just a deep moan, like from a lowing bull. But now, overwhelmed, he takes no food, no drink, sprawled in silence." His body had returned to her. She wondered when the rest would return. The answer was never. Tecmessa begs for someone to lift this burden from her husband, but it does not happen, cannot happen. Ajax is someone else now, and despairing his new monstrous self, he eventually takes his own life.

Blame is not an issue here, except perhaps in some geopolitical sense. But in terms of these lives, Ajax has not failed, the marine with the two-thousand-yard stare is not too weak, and the son of the dairyman is not a monster. It is war—brutality beyond what we can reasonably absorb—that is to blame.

Wives from Tecmessa's day until now have wished that they could say the thing that would let their men go back to "before," that would put everything back where it belonged, where the men they loved were not sprawled in silence or off someplace two thousand yards away. I know, as these wives know, that wishing will not return life to "before." "Before" is forever gone.

When my son Wade died, I spent so many days or weeks or months trying to find a way to make it not so, to have him live. The American poet Edna St. Vincent Millay writes of this desire in her lovely poem "Interim": "How easily could God, if He so willed, set back the world a little turn or two! Correct its griefs, and bring its joys again!" That's all we want. A little turn or two. And Wade is alive, and the cancer is gone, and my husband turns away from the ludicrous words "You are so hot." Just a turn and all these things can go away and we can go back to having a freckled son. Just a turn and the ninety-some years that my grandmothers lived will be mine, too. Just a turn and the misery of having your past and your future taken away by something so unpleasant as a woman with nothing but idle time to spend hanging around outside fancy hotels would be avoided.

But we cannot, they cannot turn back. This is the life we have now, and the only way to find peace, the only way to be resilient when these landmines explode beneath your foundation, is first to accept that there is a new reality. The life the army wife knew before her husband went to war, the life of the patient before the word "terminal" was said aloud, the life of the mother who sat reading by her son's bed and not his grave, these lives no longer exist and the more we cling to the hope that these old lives might come back, the more we set ourselves up for unending discontent.

Each time I fell into a chasm—my son's death or a tumor in my breast or an unwelcome woman in my life—I had to accept that the planet had taken a few turns and I could not turn it back. My life was and would always be different, and it would be less than I hoped it would be. Each time, there was a new life, a new story. And the less time I spent trying to pretend that Wade was alive or that my life would be just as long or that my marriage would be as magical, the longer I clung to the hope that my old life might come back, the more I set myself up for unending discontent. In time, I learned that I was starting a new story. I write these words as if that is the beginning and end of what I did, but it is only a small slice of the middle, a place that is hard to reach and, in reaching it, only a stepping-off place for finding or creating a new life with our new reality. Each time I got knocked down, it took me some time just to get to acceptance, and in each case, that was only part of the way home.

We all want a personal story line with a happy ending, understanding that in some abstract way it has to be punctuated periodically by some grief and heartache. Oh my goodness, did I want it. I was the heroine in every book; I was the poet; I was the singer or the one to whom every song was sung. I was, by any measure, ridiculous in the way I insisted that my life would be some idealized story, unachievable not only in life but in anything but the most saccharine of fiction. And in my story, the inevitable griefs could not be permanent and the unavoidable heartaches had to be curable by a corrected misunderstanding or by some perfect tenderness that thoroughly erases all pain. We so desperately want a map that lays out in serene pastels the paths our lives are supposed to take that we create them, we gravitate to them, we embrace and internalize them, all to no good end, for as my friend Gordon Livingston says, when the map does not comport with the ground, the map is wrong. In my life, the map has almost always been wrong.

We will each have hardships that are more difficult than we imagined we could ever face. I have cancer. It consumes my life in ways I cannot control. Long after my initial treatments, my hands and feet are still numb, the general numbness disturbed only by a tight and constant tingling. My hair, once perhaps the most reliable of my features, is thin and sparse, and I see no real prospect of that changing. My schedule is now and always will be determined by infusion appointments and MRIs. Every Christmas is my last well Christmas, or it could be.

When the Maytag plant closed in Newton, Iowa, in October 2007, the last of the four thousand workers who had once worked for Maytag in Newton, whose parents and grandparents had worked for Maytag, left the plant that had been the center of life in Newton for 114 years. The plant was known as a place where everyone was family. When there was a death or a divorce, they all shared the pain. When someone's son went off to war, all their sons were leaving and they grieved and worried as one. And when there were good days, they would play softball or have water fights in the summer or work all night when they were snowed in, as they were in the winter of 1973. So ingrained was their job with their community and their sense of being that they called themselves Maytagers. It was who they were, and then, because of global economic forces or because of the notion of an executive who did not know them or the willingness of someone half a world away to work for wages that could not feed you in Newton, Iowa, it all ended. Some of them could see it coming, like a malignancy, but they didn't know when it would kill the Maytager in them. All they knew is that one day it would and there was nothing they could do about it.

That last day, some of the Maytagers unlaced their work boots, placed them neatly side by side, and walked to their cars in their socks, their boots symbolizing what they were leaving behind, the part that could not come with them on the next part of their journey. The boots would be now—and for as long as Maytag could stand the image—lined up together by the plant door as the Maytagers once had been. It was, in a sense, like they had left the map of what their life was supposed to be at the place where the map no longer comported with the ground. The gesture was sad and angry and beautiful. The Maytagers mostly got other jobs, some better, some worse, but maybe none with the magic of history and family they had once had. And Newton got a racetrack and other employers, and now living in Newton is still good, but it is different. The longer a Maytager sat pining for what he had lost, the more lost he became. Sometimes we have to give ourselves space to grieve what we have lost: a person, a way of life, a dream. But at some point we have to stand up and say, this is my new life and in this life I need a new job.

I suppose that in real life, we have to distinguish between those catastrophes we can repair and those that require us to face a new reality. John and I used to be "fixers." If there was a problem, we would put all our energy behind fixing it, for ourselves or our families or friends, even for children who played on the sports teams we coached. No problem was too small or too large. If you work hard enough you can fix anything—or so we thought. And not just "could"—we had to. We were, we believed, obligated to right things, and so we did. And then Wade died, and we could not control the very most important thing in our lives. Accepting that this catastrophe was not vulnerable to our will was nearly impossible. Finding ways to make the erasure of this boy not so complete was all we could accomplish now. A new reality, considerably less good than the one we had before he died.

Eight years later, I had arranged my life around my new story. It would always be a central fact of my life that I was the mother of a dead boy, but it was not the only fact. My husband was in the United States Senate, my oldest daughter was in college, and I was sufficiently healthy to have had two more children. But not healthy enough. In 2004, I found out I had cancer. I determined to be a model patient so that breast cancer would just be a chapter in my new Wade-less life. And for a while it seemed to have worked; the treatments yielded what looked like a good result. But less than three years later, the cancer came back. This time it was incurable. No amount of being the obedient patient was going to change that. I could not control my own body. I still do what the doctors tell me to do. I still hope, perhaps without reason, that if I am very, very good, I will get to live and one day watch my youngest graduate from high school and one day hold my grandchild. Despite my hopes I understand that rogue cells inside my body have more control over my fate than I have. My new reality.

Last year my husband told me of an indiscretion, and my sense of what I meant to the people around me was, to put it lightly, shaken. We had, I believed, a great love story, bound as we were by triumph and defeat, by exhilarating achievement and shattering grief. We had walked side by side for three decades and in my foolish dreams would walk side by side, hand in hand, for three more. But even if my illness somehow allows me those days, they will by necessity be different because, at the very least, I am a different person now. I was not wounded, not afraid, not uncertain before, and now I always will be. He can try to treat the wound, and he has tried. He can try to make me less afraid, and he has tried. But I am now a different person. I am the Army wife, too, with a husband I don't quite know, and I have to accept him, if I can, with the new scars—many self-inflicted—which he now bears. The way we were is no longer the way we can be. A new reality. Maybe a new life.

Let's start with the unavoidable fact: If I had special knowledge about how to avoid adversities, about how to spot the pitfalls of life, I would spot them, I would avoid them, and I would share how it is I have managed that. I do not. I have a lot of experience in getting up after I have been knocked down, but clearly, I do not know anything at all about avoidance. We all tumble and fall. I certainly have, but in truth it is going to happen, in some degree, to all of us. Oh, maybe everyone we care about will live to attend our funerals. Maybe disease will never make you afraid of a curling iron burn. Maybe everyone whom you love and who loves you will be loyal to you in every way for every day of your life. Or maybe not.

CHAPTER 4
Toshiko

Toshiko placed the samisen in front of me. My sister Nancy and I were kneeling on the floor of our quarters on the Marine Corps Air Facility at Iwakuni, Japan. Toshiko was kneeling in front of us. Toshiko had promised that when I was ready I could learn to play the instrument. And here it was in front of me. The body was a little less wide than long, slightly larger than a banjo. The neck was polished sandalwood. Just three strings, one thicker than the next, stretched from the neck over a buffalo horn bridge to the catskin-covered body. It was simple and beautiful. Next to the samisen she placed a plectrum, or pick. It was sandalwood with ivory at the wide end, and nearly eight inches long. I reached to touch it, but Toshiko's hand reached mine before mine reached the plectrum. Her motion told me to be patient, and as if to show me how, she sat perfectly still for what seemed like five minutes to a nine-year-old girl.

Patience was something at which Toshiko excelled. She had left her home in Hiroshima when she was ten years old, about the age I was when she first placed the samisen before me. She traveled to Kyoto, to the narrow streets of the Gion Kobu district, to begin her training as a geisha. Someone, perhaps her mother, knew that the ten-year-old would grow to be a beautiful woman, with a serene face and delicate features. And knew, too, that these gifts of beauty, serenity, and delicacy could make her a sought-after geisha. The first months in training would be a disappointment, surely, as she served as a maid in the household in which she lived. The most tedious chores would be saved for her, a test of her determination, her work ethic. She studied dance and art and the samisen in the morning, worked in the household in the day, and attended to a geisha returning from a night's work sometimes into the early-morning hours. She would have to wait through these months before developing enough skill to become a maiko, an apprentice geisha. But patience was something at which Toshiko excelled.

Toshiko studied in the famous Fujima-Ryu system, one of the most rigorous courses of training, but one that would, with her beauty, allow her to be one of the top geishas. Over the years, she perfected her dance, her samisen playing, her conversational skills. She planned to leave Gion and join her sister in Tokyo as a full-fledged geisha, with the world in front of her, but first she would return home to her parents in Hiroshima. It was a mild August of 1945, an excellent time for travel.

Toshiko had been home for two days when, as she arose, she heard the sound of a general alarm throughout her hometown. There had been alarms before in the industrial city, warnings that American bombers might be approaching, but Hiroshima had largely been spared from any bombings. No one was surprised when shortly later the all-clear sounded. Toshiko had waited for the all-clear before leaving to go to the market. August was the month in which schools were not in session, and Toshiko walked past children working at their family store or playing in the alleyways. She was turned back to look at a stickball game in an alley she passed when she was knocked to the ground. It was as if a huge, dense, overwhelming wall of heat had raced down the street and knocked her and everyone around her to the dirt. Or it seemed so, as those like her looked back on it. It was probably hours later that she regained consciousness. Her clothes had been ripped away and her chest and arms were covered with loose charred skin. Her hair was burned away in the back, since she had turned her head to watch the children when the force of the first atomic bomb used in warfare hit her body. She could see only a gray soup of soot and smoke around her, and she could hear the sounds of people moving, wailing, or calling for help. Weakly, she closed her eyes again.

After months of treatment, Toshiko was able to return to a somewhat normal life. But it could never be the life for which she had planned and trained for a decade. Her hair had grown back and her face was largely unscarred, but her chest had literally been blown off. The scars crept nearly up to her neck and would have shown in the open neckline of the fine kimonos she had acquired as a maiko. The burns made her arms look like the arms of a ninety-year-old woman, and the pattern of the kimono she was wearing that morning was, in places, burned into them. Keloids that looked like smooth boils grew in places on the scars. A geisha was the meeting of a beautiful woman with the skills of dance and the arts. A man in conversation with her was to be flattered, not only in words but by the mere presence of this exquisite creature. And Toshiko, to say the least, was no longer exquisite.

The life that she had expected, filled with luxuries, prestige, and stimulation, was not going to be. The skills she had so diligently acquired had little value in her new life. Toshiko did begin to teach dance, but there was not much demand in postwar Hiroshima. The American military base that opened on the site of the Japanese air station in Iwakuni provided a new opportunity in the mid-1950s. Young women from Hiroshima found work there as maids and seamstresses in the homes of military families. Toshiko let a friend who worked there tell her employer that she was available to teach Japanese dance to the American children who lived there.

My mother heard about Toshiko and contacted her. Would she be willing to teach a seven-year-old and a nine-year-old? Toshiko agreed and began coming each week to our house on the base. It was an hour trip from Toshiko's home in Hiroshima to our home in Iwakuni. She would walk to the train station in Hiroshima, ride to Iwakuni station, and take the bus to the gate near our quarters.

Hiroshima would now always be home to Toshiko. The people of Hiroshima had all been through the horrors of the atomic bomb, and they all wore scars, physical or emotional, as a result. It was, I suppose, the only place where she could now feel at home. In E. Annie Proulx's brilliant novel *The Shipping News,* the main character, Quoyle, is a "damp loaf of a body" who is out of place his whole life until he returns to his ancestral home in Killick-claw, Newfoundland, a community inhabited by people as rough around the edges as the harsh landscape. There, he is not out of place; there, the physical or emotional eccentricities that would make the people around him misfits elsewhere are almost unseen. What is visible is their basic decency. Quoyle has found a place where his abnormality is invisible. Toshiko had done the same.

For our first dance lesson, my sister and I dressed in silk kimonos my mother had bought. Mine was red with yellow and white chrysanthemums; Nancy's was orange with blue and white cherry blossoms on it. We each wore red butterfly obi belts with pretied obi bows, and on our feet odori tabis, the white cotton socks with clasps and a hard sole worn by Japanese dancers, and our new vinyl getas. Mother put our hair up in buns so that we could wear these huge hairpins we had bought at a Japanese market. They had a cluster of colored umbrellas from which hung silver-colored spangles. Toshiko came in a blue and white yukata, a cotton kimono, and a simple date-jime woven belt as her obi. Even we knew to feel a little foolish. In subsequent lessons, we still wore the silk kimonos and butterfly obi belts, as they were all we had, but the hairpins did not reappear.

If our dress seemed outlandish to a woman who had done household chores in her first days of training in dance, she did not show it. In our living room, she showed little reaction or emotion at all. Perhaps it was her training, perhaps it was her nature, or perhaps it was her acceptance that this was now her life, teaching the children of an American military pilot in 1958 the skills she had learned and, because of another American military pilot in 1945, she could never use.

It was not, however, that she was simply gritting her teeth and doing what she needed to live. I have a letter she wrote to my mother, offering to take us to the Iwakuni Bon Odori festival so we could join with Japanese children in dance. She offered to teach me to play the samisen and for the first lesson brought her own samisen. And she sat behind me as I tried to play, putting her arms around me more gently than the drape of a robe on your shoulders and showing me where on the instrument my hand should be. In the pauses in the music she would place her hands over mine to still them. There was no written music for the samisen, so the only way to learn was for someone trained in the ancient art to share the music with you. And Toshiko, disfigured by an American bomb, was sharing it with me. It was a gift the value of which I only later understood when Toshiko taught me the notes she had learned in Gion.

Each week, she would share what she had spent a decade learning. She would position our legs so that two awkward American girls could appear, for a moment, graceful. We would fidget, we would fall off the sides of the heeled getas, we would try to make each other laugh when Toshiko was showing us how to rise from a kneeled position or how to close a dance fan in a single motion. She would pretend she didn't notice when our eyes settled on the

scars in the V of the yukata's neckline. She was in all
things a picture of patience and dignity.

In the two years that I knew Toshiko, I remember her smiling slightly, her lips closed and the corners of her mouth turning up, while she nodded her
head when we accomplished some skill she had been
teaching. Aside from that, I do not remember any
signs of joy. I never heard her laugh, but I never saw
her frown.

After she left that first lesson, Nancy and I
asked about the scars we had seen on her arms re-
vealed by the yukata's wide sleeves and on her chest.
Mother told us what they were. We had been to Hiroshima; we had seen the devastation. We were not
allowed to go to the museum that showed the inju-
ries and the dead, but we heard about it from our
friends. And we saw on the streets of Hiroshima the
scars of the living. Great keloid mountains of scarring across the face of a young man, an old woman
whose wrinkles and scars formed a dense plaid of
lines across her cheeks. The story of what really
happened in Hiroshima had been kept quiet for a
decade, so many of the injured had not gotten
needed medical attention. And many of the children
who had been born since that August were born

with deformities. In some ways, the tale of the living on the streets was, I suspect, more moving than the tale of the dead in the museum.

We do what we can. We make plans and prepare for the life we dream could be. And maybe for some it happens, but it didn't happen for Toshiko. She, like I, salvaged the parts she could and put them together as well as she knew how. There is, I believe, a happy ending to Toshiko's story. She accepted her life as it was. If she bore resentment or hatred, she found a way to bury it, to not let it define the rest of her life. And she found the happiest ending now available to her in the pleasures of a simple life, the dignity of her remarkable civility and the absence of pain. There was a serenity to her acceptance that was noble and strong and heartbreaking.

I no longer have the samisen my mother bought me when I learned my first song. The sandalwood and ivory pick sits on a table in my back hall. I cannot remember the notes that Toshiko taught me or the steps to the dances. But the lessons I learned from her will always be with me.

CHAPTER 5

1996

When our son Wade died in 1996, I wrote a short essay about his life and his death.

> *Wade was 16 when he died. On April 4th, 1996, the wind blew across a North Carolina field and pushed his car slightly off the road. Slightly but enough. When he tried to bring it back on, the car flipped. The air bag came out, the seat belt held, but the roof collapsed on him. The other boy walked away. Some dishes he was taking to the beach for us were unbroken. Our boy was killed instantly. It wasn't speed, it wasn't inattention, it was a straight road on a clear afternoon, and it simply was.*
>
> *And what that wind took at Easter was a cherished boy, a remarkable child with the character of a man. I try to find, in this narrow place, a way to explain his virtues. He was a loving son*

and brother, holding our hands, hugging us, no matter who was around to see. He was a loyal friend, always there when his friends needed him, but never succumbing to peer pressure. He never drank or smoked. When a parent who came on the accident asked if drinking was involved, the boys there all answered, "Wade Edwards? No way." He usually drove home those who did drink. He was intelligent and determined. His conversation in the car that day was about how he wanted to be a lawyer, but he didn't want to take anything from his parents, he wanted to do it all himself, like his father had. He was humble and shunned the spotlight. During the week before he died, his English class studied "The Snows of Kilimanjaro" by Ernest Hemingway. He participated in four days of discussion but never mentioned once that he had climbed Kilimanjaro with his father the previous summer. How many among us could have sat quietly? He went to Washington as one of ten national winners of an essay contest two weeks before he died. He did not even tell his closest friends, who only later saw him on television. He was fair-minded. When asked on Martin Luther King Day how we could

*make the world a better place, he answered,
"Look at the inside of people, not the outside." He
was seven years old when he wrote that. Though
he had many gifts, he never thought of himself
as the tiniest bit better than anyone else. And he
chastised those who treated others poorly.*

*I have tried to think about the nature of the
bond between us. I guess the fact of "bond" as-
sumes we are two people, such as would need a
bond to hold them together. And I never really
felt that degree of separateness that lets you describe the existence of a bond between two different things. His joys were my joys, his pains were
multiplied to be my pains. I woke to him and slept
only after his lips grazed mine. As private as he
held some details of his life, protecting those he
cared about from my judgment, his broader life
was open, bare before me. I was the witness to all
things he valued, most of which were intangible.
His weakness, his strength, his vulnerability (which
had worried me so), his sense of who he was and
what this living business was all about, he laid
that open. The truth of life, I would have guessed,
could not be found out in sixteen years, and we
would be fortunate to have a glimpse in sixty.*

Somehow, this child knew. Knew that we all fought too much over foolishness, that our vanity and our insecurities kept us from truly helping one another, that true love and friendship were marked by humility and loyalty that disregarded self-interest. And he more than knew these things, he lived this way. His mark will endure, because only these truths of life do endure. The good we do really is eternal, as we had told him, and now that axiom is a charge to us—not just to keep his memory, but to live his life message.

We know that we can never make sense of his loss. He had done it all right. Of all he wanted, he wanted most to be a father someday. And what an unbelievable father he could have been with his compassion, his warmth, his patience. He was a rare gift.

He wrote in a journal during Outward Bound when he was 15: "More than any other goal that I have set for myself I want to show my love and appreciation to my family for all that they have done for me. I know that I don't deserve all that I get but I hope that I will someday be able to say that I deserve it. I really want to do something great with my life. I want to start a family when

*I grow up. I am going to be as good a parent to
my kids as my parents are to me. But more than
anything, when I die, I want to be able to say that
I had a great life. So far I have had a wonderful
life and I hope it keeps up." Well, it didn't keep up
as long as it should have, but we are thankful for
what he left us. And he left everyone he touched
the better for knowing him. We stand a little
straighter in his shadow.*

❧

Nothing of any size or duration is as magical as our
memory of it. The way my mother laughed once at
something my father said when we were driving
in the rain forest in Puerto Rico, first a deep, full,
long laugh, then with remnants of the laughter low
and hearty coming out in little bits for the minutes
following. It was perfect and beautiful, sexy even
I suppose, although that is harder to say about
one's mother. The trip itself? Not so perfect. It was
Christmas, and I wanted the smell of Douglas fir in
the living room, not the absence of any smell from a
fake miniature tree mother had packed in her suitcase and set up in the rented living room. My brother
was dreadfully unhappy about traveling at Christmas and sulked the entire trip; the photographs of

him now make us laugh because he was so committed to not smiling for a solid week. But when we tell the story of it, we tell of the funny trip through the rain forest and a clever mother who packed a tree in a suitcase and a focused teenager who, whatever delights we placed before him, never once smiled. And it seems perfect; at least the ten-minute version of the weeklong trip seems perfect.

Another family trip, to the mountains of Pennsylvania, was intended to be idyllic. A high school graduation trip for me—with family. My brother brought a friend, Tom Rief; my sister brought a friend, Harriet Windley. I, fortunately, did not bring anyone. The place my father had chosen, from a classified advertisement in the *Washington Post,* was a "serene three bedroom mountain cabin overlooking a meadow" for a mere $75 a week. Even in 1967, this low price should have been a warning. We loaded the girls in one car, with the food, and the boys in the other car, with the dog—who threw up the whole way, an omen of things to come. When we reached the serene cabin, it was just an old clapboard farmhouse in need of paint across from its burned-out barn, and the meadow was a pasture shared with loud, skittish cows (making the dog quite happy) that led down a slope to the visible and busy inter-state highway. Look out the front door and there was the black carcass of the barn. Look out the back door and there was the interstate. We did every activity the town and the neighboring borough had to offer—dancing at the firehouse (the only male who approached us to dance had two abscessed front teeth), skating at the roller rink (the fellow with whom I skated thought California was closer to Virginia where we lived than Virginia was to Pennsylvania), and going to the movies (where the seven of us accounted for more than three-quarters of the audience). So we spent most of the vacation at the farmhouse, listening to "The Arkansas Traveler" from the farmhouse's old 78 RPM records—the only music—and watching the wheelchair in which my mother, who had broken her ankle the day before my high school graduation, sat roll uncontrollably down the uneven floor to crash into the sink. Up-stairs our preoccupation was killing an unending stream of flies. Even this truly miserable vacation—we couldn't make it the whole week—takes on a luster. Far from perfect, perhaps, but solar systems better than the seemingly unending misery of the real thing.

So maybe it is not surprising that my sense of life before 1996 is radiant. Braiding Cate's hair or finding a Jams shirt for Wade, making mock science tests for them, cleaning the playroom with them to a silly song I made up, watching them wrap Christmas presents for each other and watching them enjoy seeing their brother or sister unwrap what they had chosen, the first time they got up on skis, the spelling bee. It is easy enough to think that those days must have been magical and perfect. The ten-minute version is undeniably perfect. We had a picture-postcard family in a picture-postcard house, and life had played out precisely as I had dreamed it would. And in my house, I literally walked around singing the songs of Jo Stafford and the Andrews Sisters.

We had enough money that we didn't have to worry so much about our mortgage or whether the car needed new wheel bearings, but we hadn't had enough money (or hadn't had it long enough) to think that hiring people to manage our lives made any sense, so it was just the four of us, at dinner, at basketball games, at soccer practice, trimming the tree. A beautiful foursome with a golden retriever to boot. A husband I adored, a life that I thought challenged him professionally and a home that fed him emotionally, and these unspeakably marvelous children. It was perfect, and I was content in my memory of life before Wade died. But to let myself fall into that fiction is not fair to today. Today will always fall short of perfection, just as yesterday— we might not remember—did.

What was perfect then that cannot be replaced is that Wade was here, a six-foot, freckle-faced, living, breathing boy whose being was one of a handful of things that made my life make sense every single day. There is nothing in life I have done better than to parent my children. And even that is not particularly close to perfect. There is always someone who parents better, who does whatever you think you can do at least a little better than you, and maybe more than a little better. Isn't that always so? There is only one person at a time who holds a world record. There is one Miss Universe a year. One winner of the Nobel Peace Prize and one for the Scripps Spelling Bee. Only a handful of winners of the Fields Medals. And I want to be clear: I was not ever going to win as best parent. In my skewed memory everything is close to perfect, but even rose-colored-glasses me remembers some realities. My house, perennially piled high with half-finished projects, looked more like Fred Sanford's living room from *Sanford and Son* than like Bree Van De Kamp's from *Desperate Housewives*. I am lucky if my kitchen smells like Sara Foster's twice a year. My freezer has more food in it than my fresh vegetables bin. My children get cavities and my older daughter came home from camp once with a hair knot the size of a Bubba Burger. I have missed the sign-up deadline for sports teams and I have sent my daughter to auditions without the sheet music every other mother handed their child as they got out of the car. I always made dinner for the mother of a new baby, but I was never the one who thought to organize it.

And yet I am, more because I am the one who raised them than that I had some extraordinary skill, the very best mother for my children, and because they raised me, they are the very best children for me. I'd like to think, perhaps deceiving myself, that my imperfections actually taught them a few things, too. I do know that I happily built my days around them, working at my law office only until school was out and then coming home, being there for homework or car pools or sewing a button on a favorite shirt. Or just being there. So the days must have been perfect, right? And then the halcyon days came to an end. The fall is much farther if you think you have fallen all the way from heaven.

When Wade died, all that imperfectly remembered perfection came crashing down. Although it wasn't perfect, and so it wasn't some large perfect world that came crashing down. What did happen was bad enough.

⁂

I remember sitting on the plane from Boston to Raleigh on the afternoon of April 4, 1996, the day Wade died. Cate and I had visited private schools to which she had been accepted. I had insisted, over her objection, she apply because she was truly gifted, particularly in mathematics, and despite my constant prodding it seemed clear the large, well-meaning public school system was not equipped to challenge her. We went to startlingly beautiful places where they were anxious for her to attend, where the students were intimidatingly bright, and where spring was popping with promise. She had to love it, right? But she didn't, and the trip was far from perfect. It was like pulling a leashed puppy across a street; there was nothing elegant or pleasant about it. She didn't want to go, and though I didn't want her to leave me, I didn't want to fail her either by having her stay home when she deserved this kind of stimulation. So here we were; the trip was over but we were still tense sitting next to each other on the flight home.

Fortunately, the flight would be followed by a family spring-break trip to the beach and then her cousin's wedding in Key West, and maybe this tension would be broken. Unfortunately, or what I thought at the time was the most unfortunate part of my day, a young family sat behind us on the plane and while the mother tended to a crying baby, the father read a newspaper, and the son, nonstop, kicked the back of my seat. Hard. How silly of me, I now know, to get agitated about such a small insult. Even without Wade's death it would have been silly. At home, I would see my husband and we would travel to the beach, where our son had gone earlier in the day. The sun would shine, we would go boating, pick shells on the beach. But as the boy kicked and the father read on, I was agitated nonetheless, and I stayed that way, complaining to Cate and then continuing to complain to John when he picked us up at the airport. I suspect I complained all the way home about the ill-behaved child and the oblivious father. But within minutes, those two were gone. They were instantly replaced when a couple of Highway Patrol cars pulled into our driveway with the news that changed every day after that day, the news that Wade was dead.

Each moment of hearing the news is etched into me. I feel the cool wind as a warm afternoon is pierced by the beginning of evening. I see, first through the window, the troopers pull into our driveway, rows of blooming daffodils hidden behind their cars as they crested the hill to the house, the beginning of leaves forming on the maple tree above them. The firm sound, then, of their car doors closing, *crumph, crumph*. And the front door opening before me, closing behind me as I rushed to the porch. The left spring squeaks. The trooper closest to me touches his holster and then his hat as he moves toward me. Everything is in slow motion. The evening is no longer breaking in. There is only heat, massive waves of hot panic. I speak first. Everyone else was home; it had to be Wade. Tell me he is alive.

It didn't matter how many times I said it. Wade was dead. However close to perfection we had come the week before, we were now on the other side of the world, of the universe. About halfway to the beach, the wind had caught Wade's car and pushed it off the road. He had tried to correct, and whether it was the wind or the edge of the road doesn't matter; he could not get the car safely back onto the highway, and it flipped. And flipped and flipped until he was dead. The speed limit on the road is 70 miles per hour. They estimated he was driving between 68 and 72. He was wearing his seat belt. The air bags deployed. He never drank. He didn't smoke. He didn't use drugs. He wasn't even talking on a cell phone. He was just talking about what he wanted to do when he grew up to Tyler in the front seat, Tyler who walked away with a sprained ankle from the crushed car. And now Wade wasn't going to grow up.

Nothing in life made sense if this boy could be dead. What had he done? What had we done? I had grown up in a world that made sense: My father was in the Navy, and there, there was good and there was evil, and if you were good, there were rewards, and if you were bad, there was punishment. Not only were there ranks—those who performed moved up—and medals—all good is acknowledged—it played out into the lives of Navy families. The officers had the best quarters, and the higher the rank the nicer the house. Each failure of the serviceman or his family was recorded, and opportunities would be withheld or promotions would never come. Families could be sent away, separated, if the conduct was serious. Life made sense to a young girl: Pride and shame were bookends, and with each came the consequences. But if that is the framework in which you grew up, how do you explain the death of a young sweet boy? The Old Testament is clear: In I Chronicles and in Psalms, the reward for a life well-lived is a longer life. Wade was as gentle and sweet as a boy might be, and yet he lived just sixteen years; where is God to put this right? Today made no sense at all; I had no frame of reference. How would I ever make sense of tomorrow? The world collapses, and nothing we can do makes any difference whatever. Why did we do everything right? Why did we learn? Here, now, when we need the reward and when we need the ability to move an admittedly large mountain, we discover we are totally impotent and totally without grace. We are spread on the floor, unable to stand. Resilience seemed a ludicrous word only uttered by those who had never felt so at sea.

It is really important for me to say, as I tell you

about my journey, that there is not only one road map here. Like fingerprints, there are road maps that belong to each of us. I know my own, but I would never suggest that it is the single right path. I would never suggest that there is even such thing as a single right way, or twenty-five ways, to get from Day One after the death of a child to Year Thirteen. There are things that work for a particular bereaved parent, and there are things that don't. The ones that work for me are the right ones, but just the right ones for me. It is as simple as that. It is hard enough without measuring yourself against some standard your parents or your friends think you should be achieving "by now." It is hard enough to find some balm that eases the burn for a moment without thinking someone else's balm is actually the one I should be applying. A bereaved mother is lucky if the same things that work for her also work for her husband. Just because it is right for one does not mean that it will be right for the other, and that tension makes a difficult road even more lonely. But the loneliness is not eased by doing what only makes someone else more at peace; in fact, it may create an even deeper sense of loneliness. I will tell you the story of my path, but only if you understand what it is: my path.

Life is a like a blackboard. We write on it the things we are, the things we do. We fill it up, sometimes erasing what we have grown out of. I am no longer a cheerleader, I no longer read Daphne du Maurier. I grow up and erase them, or rather replace them with new activities, new passions, new friends. And it seems, when we step back from it as we grow up, that our blackboard is as filled as it could be: I was a mother, a wife, a lawyer, and a soccer coach and a Goodwill volunteer. Write those down. Go to sports cards shows with Wade or doll shows with Cate? Write those. Mark down going with the family to watch the Tar Heels. There is my book club, and there's PTA fundraising. Decorating the beach house. Sewing a Halloween costume. But there is always a corner into which some new friend, some new dream can be tucked. There was always room to add one more thing to the board. In the spring of 1996, my board was crammed full, and I had chalk in my hand.

And then Wade died.

In an instant, all of my blackboard was erased. And for the longest time, the blackboard stood empty. Nothing that I was doing before seemed important. And nothing I might do tomorrow seemed worthy. I could not have anything that I truly wanted other than my family. So I wrote nothing at all. And I did nothing at all. Day after day was the same. I went to the cemetery, I read, eventually I wrote, I tried to be a mother to our surviving daughter, Cate.

No place that Wade had not been was of interest to me. No one who did not know him was good company for me. I didn't eat, couldn't eat and became thin, but I did not want new clothes. He hadn't seen them, so I didn't want them. I wore a dress he called my bumble-dress even when it was two sizes too large. I had a narrow life that brought no joy but in which I felt safe, where I felt his memory was safe, where he seemed in a sense to be present. I did not yet trust his constant presence in my life. How much of him slipped away today. Would the boys who crowded into our house and played basketball in the backyard remember him next year or in a decade? How many of the details of his life, how much of the sound of his laughter would I be able to hold on to in that time?

I was changed. I so often felt outside of myself: the grieving mother, the once-solicitous friend, the dutiful parent of my surviving daughter, but all as if

I am a puppeteer, stripped of the ability to evoke anything other than rudimentary motion in my puppet body. Real life is something other people had, something I once had and cannot imagine having again. The people we were are like characters in stories from a book; we are drawn to them, to their fullness and hope and happy naïveté, and yet we cannot reach them. It is nearly impossible to believe that once we were them. Where was the key that was going to put this right?

It was months later that I recognized there were no right answers, no elixir that would return me to the world where unbridled happiness was possible. Moving, not moving, being surrounded by their belongings, or being isolated from them, these are the rearrangements of the physical and cannot reach a part of us that needs redesign. What I had to face was not something present, it was something absent. And although we can escape something's presence, there is no way to escape its absence. There was no place to go where he would not also be absent. So it was easy to say, what difference does it make where I am? But in practice, there are comforts and there are burdens in each choice. I wrote to a parent who had lost a son who had done carpentry work, "If you move, you do not have to look at Chris's fret-work and molding, and yet, if you move, you do not get to look at Chris's fretwork and molding." For myself, I did not expect to move from the place where he was known, where now and again I could hear, "Yes, I remember him," or where I might pass his friends on the street.

Wade is buried in Oakwood Cemetery in Ra-leigh, beneath an oak so old that John and I together cannot reach around it. Another oak had stood closer to the grave, but a storm felled it. All will pass in time. For the first years after he died, I went daily. On bad days, I would go twice. For months John went with me and then I went alone, sitting at Wade's grave reading to him. First the Bible, then Elie Wiesel's *Sages and Dreamers,* given to me by Glenn, Wade's godfather, and finally the reading list for high school seniors, the books we would have read together had he lived for his seventeenth year. I planted a garden at his grave and Thomas Sayre carved a bench faced in Cate's words and mine. I cleaned around his grave and I cleaned the headstones of children buried near him. I needed Wade to be a part of each day. I needed to tell him when his SAT scores came in, when a short story of his won a statewide award. It may sound strange to others, but it is what I had to do. Cormac McCarthy in *The Crossing* wrote that "time heals bereavement . . . at the cost of the slow extinction of those loved ones from the heart's memory which is the sole place of their abode then or now. Faces fade, voices dim. Seize them back. . . . Speak with them." I needed him, so I did.

I wanted to believe, needed to believe that on some plane Wade also needed me still, maybe needed me even more dead than alive since he could no longer direct the impact of his life himself. He had done all he could and now it was my job, my new way of parenting him: to protect his memory. But first I had to come to terms with the fact that it was a memory, that I wasn't going to get him back by praying or wishing or standing completely still so God could turn back time and let Wade live. I won't lie to you— that is what I was waiting for, that is why I could not write on the blackboard: I had to make it as easy as possible for God, as Edna St. Vincent Millay had said, to set back the world a little turn or two. I did not want a new story; I loved my old story so.

I could not change his room at home in any way at all. His backpack sat on the floor near the chair for years. Not days or weeks, but years. Why should I move it? What would that accomplish? And if I didn't move it, if I didn't change anything, he could walk right in. Millay captured this, too: "You are not here. I know that you are gone, and will not ever enter here again. And yet it seems to me, if I should speak, your silent step must wake across the hall; if I should turn my head, that your sweet eyes would kiss me from the door." I read these words and fell into them. I cannot change the hall or his room unless I am willing to risk missing his sweet eyes kissing me from the door. That feeling—that you are waiting for him, that you need only wait and he will call or come—will not easily recede. What we know is apparently no match for what we need. All of my being said to accept my son's death, and some days I suppose I almost did. I'd seen his face, still and cold in the small morgue; I knew he was dead. And yet, it must not be true, it could not be true; love and justice have only to find a way to pry open death's fingers, I thought.

The truth, of course, is that the carousel ride—first forward in fits, then backward, only makes the ground spin and leaves us unable to walk even when the whirling stops. It is like the mocking, disturbing, contortions of the carousel in Ray Bradbury's *Sometimes Evil This Way Comes,* which Wade (and I, for I read what he read) was assigned in freshman English. And all the starts and fits and love and wishes and prayers are for naught, as no one gets what they want. In the end, every day was the same: The house was still quiet and the soil above his coffin undisturbed. The most I could wish for was the respite of sleep where logic had no dominion. I wanted him back so badly that the reasoning part of me, the part that had dominated my life until April 1996—the debater, the lawyer, the logic puzzle addict—laid down its arms, even in the daylight. I wanted my boy, and no amount of logic would stand in the way.

A friend, Phil Lister, whose lovely, brave daughter Liza finally lost her battle with leukemia, wrote:

Death Plus Time
how old is she
I don't know what to say
don't know how to add
six years alive and one year dead
six plus one
is usually seven but not now

six maybe
six plus one is six
in a year six plus two will be six
or six plus one is none

Everything on which we had counted had been turned upside down, even elementary addition, so who could say that our physics was not wrong or our biology was not wrong? I didn't need a new story line without him. He could return to us. And when he did return I wanted him to know we were waiting for him; we hadn't moved on without him. The warrior's wife not moving while he is away, not changing the setting so their story could be unchanged by war, just as mine could be unchanged by physics and biology and Phil's could be unchanged by mathematics.

I knew enough to know, though, that Phil's addition and my biology would seem unbalanced outside our sad world. So I used another logic to explain to others why I didn't move a single thing in his room. His room is what he put together, I wrote. We had gone to Washington, D.C., and looked for furniture together—an odd place to travel from North Carolina in search of furniture, but it was his

choice and his room. I let him pick what he wanted.
Since he was only sixteen when he died, he had had
the chance to put so little together, I could not bear
to take any of it apart. There was already too little of
him here on earth. People who might have thought
I was unbalanced if I said it was waiting for him to
return so I wasn't changing his room could understand that he had made the room and I wanted to
save what he had made. So no one argued when I
left his room alone. I did wonder how I would ever
get the strength to change it. Would it be the closed
door on the second floor for as long as I lived? I was
spared the test of whether I could move anything
of Wade's: a flood in the laundry room next to his
room started to spread a mildew throughout his
room, and I rushed to save the things he loved by
taking that room apart. His books, his papers, his
sports cards and trophies, his signed Michael Jordan
Wings poster—which later a dreadful someone tried
to steal, an incomprehensible violation of Wade.

It was my job to protect his things—and I did
and do—since he could not. I got his belongings
away from the mildew, I recovered the poster. But
change anything? Shoot, I still store his elementary
school project on chance and his high school project

on the infinity box. I had to take apart his room, but I could not do any more than absolutely necessary to displace the boy. It is easy to say that my husband and I and our three living children live in my house today, but it is more accurate to say that we house four children here.

I think at some level I also needed particular places in which to grieve. His room was one. I did not need it to feel close to Wade, I was feeling close to him everywhere (in part because I refused for a time to move out of his world), but his room was special, a refuge in my worst moments. When his absence came crashing in on me particularly hard, I would go there, lie on his bed, sit on the floor in front of his backpack, and ignore the reality of his absence. His backpack, just dropped off from school as it always was, just where it always sat. And his sheets with the smell of him captured beneath the comforter. I could pretend—for it was pretense, I knew at some level—that he was just gone, not dead. His room was where I could allow myself not to adjust to the new reality. This was the strongest medicine I had. Well, the strongest medicines— hallucinogens actually—were likely the videotapes of him, but I wasn't ready for them then or now.

Wade was with me everywhere, but there was no place like his unchanged room for denying that he was forever gone.

I even saw him places he clearly was not. I looked in every black Grand Cherokee, the model of car in which Wade died, hoping to find him. It had all been a mistake, I so wanted to believe. I even followed a Cherokee one day. The young driver had his arm on the rim of the open window just as Wade used to do while driving. I followed knowing it was not him but unable not to follow on the chance that God had granted my wish but only if I showed the tenacity to find Wade myself, to follow this car when it drove by.

I wanted to scream at people who were mowing their lawns or fixing their porch. Don't build that high-rise, don't paint that store. Please. My God is just about to turn back time. But I didn't scream and they mowed and hammered and painted. Like Tecmessa I wanted it to be as it had been, and it was impossible to think that this—the most important fact in my life—was invulnerable to my efforts, my prayers.

The movement of a bird on the mullion of the window, the flight of a butterfly or lightbulbs going out. The ring of the phone with no one at the other end, a shiny dime on the sidewalk. Some of us who have lost our children sometimes see them there. Not all of us see them, not all of us see them in everything, but we need them in such an enormous, encompassing way that we cannot imagine that need is not big enough to bring us something, some part of him. So we look where no one who hasn't stood where we stood would look. He had to be here, somewhere here. I looked in closets, I opened drawers. Drawers! He was six feet tall. The distorted biology of a grieving mother. I knew as I opened the drawer that he could not be there, and yet I was powerless: I had to open it. What if somehow he could be there?

And then there came a time when I did not open drawers. The illogical searching did not end, but I moved through that place where I was searching for him to a place where I knew he was not there in a drawer—anymore. (Not, I have to admit, that he couldn't have been there; simply that he was not in a drawer in my house; he had, at the very least, moved on.) It was nearly a year later when I had a dream of finding him, a dream without logic, but with drawers—drawers I could not open. I was at a beach something like Rehoboth Beach in Delaware, where we used to go with my parents. One of those idyllically remembered places, where my father would roll the children down the boardwalk in a big gardener's wheelbarrow, and we would grill corncobs and sit for hours watching the Atlantic and eating steamed crabs and grilled corn and cold beer. But it is not that Rehoboth in my dream. In this Rehoboth, I felt out of place. I am drawn to something in the distance and, knowing only that I need whatever it is, I rush toward it, down the boardwalk to the south, past the DuPont houses, to a place I have never been, where I know somehow I am not allowed. Suddenly there is an older woman beside me, and she walks me to an apartment I seem to know. Another woman meets me at the door and invites me in. She introduces me to her husband, who has no face. I am the woman, she tells him, whose nephew died, and the nephew was the same age as their son Lucky. I can see Lucky behind her and her daughter behind him. I've met them all before. I corrected her: Wade is my son.

I had been standing near the doorway in a narrow room with a linoleum table, and as we walked to the kitchen, my eyes were drawn at once to the handles on the cabinets and drawers. They were all broken in the middle and only the stumps of handles were still connected, too small to use to open the drawers. I continued to talk to the woman, and then Lucky and his sister were gone and Wade and Cate came in and stood by the linoleum table.

We spoke a little more and then left, Wade by my side, Cate wandering behind us some, looking back at the couple standing at the door. We walked and talked, and when I talked to Cate I had to turn around. When I turned back to Wade, he was climbing the steps of a bright white porch. I can help you with that, son, I said. Cate walked up with him. I knew I was not to go. I know, he said, thanks, Mom. I stood outside. Alone.

And I didn't look in drawers again. I seemed to have understood that even if there had been a time when I could have erased all that happened and have him, that time had passed and now he was going on without me.

Maybe it should have scared me a year later that he was still this enormous presence in my life and in my dreams but I felt quite the opposite: I was more distressed when he was not with me. Drawers, beaches, thin sliced ham he liked, black Grand

Cherokees, a blinking answering machine light, I
knew these were irrational triggers, but I did not
even ask myself not to respond when something
pushed a button on Wade's memory. Without them,
where was he in my life? And if, when it happened,
I was alone, I fell willingly into the grief. I think I
actually wanted it; I think I reacted to the song on
the radio or the cola on the grocery shelf as a trigger
precisely because I needed his company. It was not
a hairshirt to me the way it might have seemed to
someone outside my family; it was a warm envelop-
ing comforter, it was as close as I could be in this life
to my boy. But that comfort, I had to learn, was an
impediment to being able to live as fully as possible
after Wade's death. As long as I lived there, I wasn't
living in the present, and part of Wade's legacy
would be that in dying, he took with him part of his
mother as well, leaving half a mother for Cate.

Part of becoming functioning again was accepting what I could not do, much as my father had
done as his body failed him. I could not bring him
back, as much as I tried, as much as I prayed. I could
not let him go, which is what people who cared
about me wanted. So many people, thinking they
were taking care of me, asked if I was over Wade's

death yet. I will never be "over" it, I would tell them, and they would look back at me blankly. If I had lost a leg, I would tell them, instead of a boy, no one would ever ask me if I was "over" it. They would ask how I was doing learning to walk without my leg. I was learning to walk and to breathe and to live without Wade. And what I was learning is that it was never ever going to be the life I had before.

Not too unlike the wives welcoming home their warrior husbands, I had to adjust to a new reality. Clinging to the old reality with a living Wade was paralyzingly unattainable, and as long as I did that, I was not going learn to walk. A hundred friends, at least, came by or called or wrote to tell me that I needed to move forward, for myself, for my remaining family. What did they know? I was in pain and vulnerable to every trigger that reminded me of my boy, and they were innocent and invincible. My dearest friends and my family who loved him helped. Some knew just what to do. Gwynn and David came every night in the first months, letting us talk of Wade until we were too tired to speak; they would put us to bed and come back the next evening, Gwynn often with a dinner for us in her hands. Sally would come sit with me in Wade's room. Ellan would find reasons why I should go out, walk with her, anything to leave the house to which I was so bound. Cate gave us reasons to leave, reasons to live. Her soccer games and then her softball games, all the life she had had before and was holding on to as hard as she could.

Those less close to us tried in their way to be there for us, but they seemed like foreigners who could not speak our language. We relied on their smiles and their hugs even when their words did not, could not relate to our pain. Looking back, their compassion and presence and their memories of Wade sustained me in a way honestly I did not then understand. All I thought then was that they did not know what I had not known: They could not really understand what it meant to place your child in a casket, to stand beside it in the church, to sit beside it at the cemetery. If they couldn't tell me anything about the death of my son, who could?

I found a group of people who were as lost and miserable as I was and we helped each other find our footing and find our individual paths. I suspect there are few better examples of barely functional people than those who have just buried their children. We are fortunate just to be dressed, particularly fortunate if it is not exactly what we wore the day before. We barely eat, we don't know where to go, we don't seem to belong anywhere. Yet some of us gravitate to the Internet, and there, with a little searching, we find one another. There we have no faces, no races, no houses, no cars, no jobs, no reputations. Our children were equal, no one was smarter or faster or better-looking, none were troublemakers or lawbreakers. And there we were all equal, in a fashion. There we were all parents who have done the impossible: We have placed our child in a box and the box in the ground and we do not know what to do next. And yet we were stronger when we were with one another. I mean "with" in the important figurative sense.

Around 1991, Wade had taught me how to use the Internet. Five years later I realized he had taught me how to reach a safety net that, in his permanent absence, I would sorely need. I went online sometime after his death not knowing what I would find, not really knowing what I was seeking. But there they were: a group, more than one, actually, with a safe place and a comforting if distant empathy, a group of the bereaved looking for one another. They weren't afraid, as some of my most precious and well-meaning friends (who were helpful in different ways) were, to talk of Wade's death. Losing a child to disease or accident or an intentional act—their own or others'—is a reality from which the blessedly uninitiated understandably turn away. I did it before Wade died. I am not proud now that I never asked about the birthday or death day of the long-deceased son of a good friend, but I didn't. And I understood why others circumscribed the conversations they had with me: no talk of dead children. Wouldn't I rather talk about living Cate anyway? And part of me wanted to fall wholly into that glorious child, but I could not shed Wade, didn't want to shed him.

In this odd Internet family, everyone had lost a loved one. No one stupidly believed that by not talking about it, it wouldn't happen to them. It had already happened to them. And now death and pain and loss and grief and anger and doubt, they were already here. There is a song written by Billie Holliday, "Good Morning, Heartache." She captures, in a song grieving the loss of love, the desire to avoid the pain and the impossibility of eluding it. "Stop haunting me now, can't take it no how. Just leave me alone. I got those Monday blues, straight through

Sunday blues," she starts. And then she capitulates to it: "Might as well get used to you hangin' around, good morning, heartache, sit down." Pull up a chair.

We pulled up chairs, in front of computers all over the world, and we talked. At any hour of the day or night, there was always someone there, at their chair waiting for you. In the years since I typed my first message I have met a handful of the people with whom I shared my darkest moments and my deepest doubts. And although each one of those meetings was satisfying, an odd and wonderful reunion, I always worry, as it appears we might meet, that our in-face differences will somehow come between us. Wade, at seven, was asked, for a Martin Luther King Day celebration in school, what lesson he had learned from King. *Look at the inside of people, not the outside,* he wrote. The wish of a seven-year-old boy and now the wish of a forty-six-year-old woman. I did not want anything, like thick accents or huge tattoos, to strain or test the tender strand on which I so relied. Well, we met and we were alike sometimes and different others, and it was a comfort each time, and maybe now I would not even notice the differences. Or at least I would not care.

The communities—alt.support.grief (an Internet newsgroup), Cendra Lynn's griefnet.org (a collection of e-mail lists), Tom Golden's Web Healing pages (a discussion bulletin board)—all functioned a little the same way. A person who recently lost a loved one would post about their daughter or father or wife—an introduction—and those who had been participants for a longer period of time would respond. Many responders would mention their own loss (I found it hard not to do that), but some would merely be embracing. It took a while to write of Wade. I wanted it to be just right, to reflect the boy more than my pain, to be the tribute he deserved rather than a howl from me, and maybe, honestly, I wanted to make people want to know him. He would never again say Hello, my name is Wade. So I was doing it, and that was a pretty daunting responsibility. The paragraphs that began this chapter were the way I introduced Wade to my new community.

But sharing Wade, making certain that to the extent I was able I parented his memory as well as a mother might, that made that day easier, which made the next day easier. I created a new place for him. Just as I grew to know Wally and Michael and Christian, Lucas and Liza and Chase, their grieving parents grew to know Wade, or the version of Wade I showed them. And there, frankly, he was a nearly perfect boy. And there, I could be less than a perfect mother and less than a perfect grieving mother and still feel safe. The central premise of the groups, which was largely but not entirely honored, is that we protected one another. Anyone could ask anything or express a fear or expose an indiscretion without fear of being criticized. We all knew the new boundaries of our existence. Everything was safe. It was more than therapeutic; it was a new home where Wade's memory had a place.

In this wholly ethereal world where no one had a physical presence, I could accept his physical absence—in a way—and I could parent his memory, keeping that a central part of who I was. In this community, it was all I was: Wade's mother. A decade later, I talked to Astrid, Christian's mother. What have you been doing? she asked. I paused. Astrid didn't know anything about me beside Wade. I quit practicing law, I started. You were a lawyer? We have had two more children. My husband ran for the senate. The state senate? No, the

U.S. Senate. He won, and we moved to Washington. That must have been interesting; are you still there? I paused again. No, we are back in North Carolina. He ran for vice president instead of his Senate seat. He lost, and we are back home. Now the silence belonged to Astrid. Astrid told me later she went to Christian's grave and spoke to him. You will not believe, Christian, who Wade's father is. In our Internet community, he was Wade's father and I was Wade's mother. The world outside demands that we be lawyers or bus drivers or teachers or senators. Here all we needed to be was mothers and fathers.

All I wanted to be was a mother. A mother to Wade and as much of a mother as I could manage being to Cate, who was then just fourteen. I stopped being a lawyer; I never went back after the accident and I have never looked back at that decision with any regret. It seemed to me that it had nothing whatever to do with Wade, so I left. But it meant that my days, once full, were pretty empty. People who cared about me tried to fill them, tried to provide solace, mostly in activities that had nothing to do with Wade—sweetly, they wanted me to move away from the grief, I suppose.

There was a long time, though, when I would brush off solace. Maybe I didn't want to move away from the pain. Maybe it was not wanting to rewrite my life without him, or maybe it was what Edmund Wilson, the incomparable twentieth-century literary critic, said. Why should I have solace when he hasn't breath? Wilson wondered how he could be expected to enjoy what life offers when what life offers had been denied to one as substantial and serious and dear as his wife. That is how I felt about Wade. I get solace, a balm for me, and there is nothing whatever for him? I can understand on some rational level that the pleasure we take from life cannot diminish our children's pleasure, but there will always be with that logic an unstated reservation: that our children should have this pleasure as well, or instead of us. But our children weren't going to have pleasure, because they weren't going to live. And so I tried, as much as possible, not to live too much either. Or at least not live for me.

I pressed my life, my hopes into a dogwood tree at his elementary school, a scholarship in his name, a bench at his high school, finally a whole computer lab. See it? See him? Don't let him pass unnoticed through this life. John went on to do things, back to the courtroom, back to work that made a difference for living people. I was still there, still at the cemetery, still at the computer lab, still in his bedroom.

These gestures that kept his presence in the lives of those who knew him also did something else. Little by little, it became easier to accept Wade's death, because I had something to parent in his place. I had someplace else where he would be, in a sense.

On the suggestion of a friend, Gene Hafer, John and I decided to start a computer lab for high school students in his name. It never occurred to us how ambitious the project was. If we had known, perhaps we would have shied away, but we didn't know and so we threw ourselves into it. Finding the location across from his high school, raising the money, doing the renovation, getting the computers and the staff, filled every day for months. And then I would go there, parent the children who were using the lab, tell them a search engine hint Wade had taught me, and it was as close to him as I could ever be again without my nose between the sheets of his now-empty bed or in the grass above his grave. The computer lab was more than a place, though; I was doing something, actively parenting his memory. You don't, I discovered, leave the need to parent the child just because the child has left you. So doing something meant I had a way to do that.

I wasn't alone either, and knowing that was important. Among our online community Lana planted a garden for her daughter Brooke; Bill was father to Michael and guide to all newcomers at alt.support. grief. The Internet itself gave parents a place to parent, and in the years that I spent as part of the grief community, hundreds of Web sites and thousands of individual Web pages came online, each a lifeline for a lonely parent. I visit them still, and in each one, I see the mother choosing the pictures, writing just the words she hopes will capture her child and will introduce her to those people she never got a chance to meet. I did it, too. I posted where I could; when the computer lab opened, I worked on a Web page for the Wade Edwards Learning Lab, and no page was more important to me than the one that awkwardly, sweetly I hope, told the visitor who Wade Edwards was.

But I also found that for me and for other parents, doing these things was not complete insulation. Sometimes I felt the same emptiness even while I was doing the things that kept his memory alive. It was as if some aching part of me was screaming at the part of me doing the remembering: *What are you doing, treating this child as dead?* It is a cruel result that the few things we can do for our children are also the things that sometimes intensify the sense of loss. When we got the building we had wanted for the computer lab across from his high school, it should have been a great day. It meant that the "Wade Edwards Learning Laboratory" would be in place in the fall. Matt Leonard, who had climbed Mount Kilimanjaro with Wade and his father a year before, was already planning how to turn the space into a computer lab. Everything was falling into place. And yet somehow the news that the lab would soon be real also had its hard edge. "Memorial." "Dead."

It is always there. Sometimes the most present thing of all is his absence. I close my eyes and see his lips and his breath across them. I shut out all the noise and hear his laughter in the next room. What was therapy yesterday is simply painful today. And I have to let that happen. I cannot pretend that I can't hear that laughter somewhere distant from me. But it is precisely because I let myself hear it today, because I let myself cry today, that tomorrow I can paint the walls in the lab. And each day, sadly, it is a little less likely that I hear that laughter. (I think, honestly, that one of the reasons I cannot watch the videotapes is that they would relight that voice I love and fear.)

Grief is a long process of untangling ourselves from the physical reality of the person and from our expectations of our future with them. I knew a girl in college named Laura Del Maestro. Some years before she came to college, her house in New Jersey had burned down; everything in it was destroyed. She told me that her family had grieved for what they had lost and moved to a new home, the grieving, they thought, behind them. But it wasn't. Some holiday or some old friend or some seemingly benign comment would trigger a memory, and they would grieve a loss they hadn't realized they had suffered. Something else had burned that they hadn't remembered at first. It is like that when you lose someone with whom you have expectations of a long future. When the late fall came after Wade died, we received in the mail our season tickets to the University of North Carolina basketball games. What had been an exciting moment every year before that was like a dagger: How can I possibly go? How can I enjoy the games he so loved without him?

The process continues for me today as his friends marry. These are boys—now young men—whom I dearly love, and they are experiencing one of the great joys of life, but I cannot go and tell them how happy I am for them. This is yet something else that burned in the fire, a loss I had not wrapped myself around in 1996. So now, with each wedding, it wraps itself around me. Even though it gives me pain, my feelings about it are unambiguous. I am the mother of a dead son and a living daughter. As the mother of a dead boy, I want Wade's memory to be a part of their lives, but I recognize, as much as it hurts, that it is but memory, that he is dead. As the mother of a living daughter, I want them to know that honoring his memory does not mean limiting their joys; they honor him most by valuing the fullness of life. It was a lesson I was having trouble applying to myself.

In the moments when I felt at loose ends—the wedding of a close friend of Wade's, Christmas and birthdays, high school graduations, the death of another child—all the work I felt I had done to come to terms with Wade's absence seemed to evaporate. In those moments, I turned, as I did so often in those days, to my fellow travelers, those struggling with the same kinds of moments, trying to keep their balance now that the world around them was so disarranged. I turned to the Internet.

It is hard to overstate what the online grief community meant to me. We helped one another with the smallest of things—do you buy a Christmas gift for the staff at the cemetery?—to how we were going to manage living at all after the death of one we cherished. In my first weeks in the community, I met Gordon Livingston, whose son Lucas had had leukemia. Gordon sent me his book, *Only Spring,* about Lucas's struggle against the disease and Gordon's attempt to save him. After I finished the book, I tried to write to Gordon to tell him what his book meant to me.

I turned the last page of Only Spring yesterday morning, my mind racing with your children and mine, with your despair and my own. I carried them with me yesterday, trying to imagine how to write you. And with me last night, and with me today. My fingers still, unable to write. And now, I write because I need to, not because I have matched words with my reaction to your words and to your children.

The closest I can come is to tell you how real Lucas seems to me. There was no mystery; I knew the end. I did not know, however, how I would feel about him as I read. If I could reach across time—oh, if that were only possible—I wanted to reach across and pull him over those last days to safety. I had thought how hard it was to never have the chance to say goodbye to Wade, to only think back on his last words, his last touch. I had thought how I wished I could have had that—except, of course, if it came at such a price as Lucas and you, and Clare and Emily paid. I don't know how you start the awful journey after death spent so much of you all.

The image of Lucas on the ride at Rehoboth Beach has stayed with me most persistently. I am certain it is because for so many years we went every summer to my parents' place there. The garden cart in which my father pushed Wade and his sister Cate and his cousin Jordan down the boardwalk sits empty in my garage now. A photograph of him running on the boardwalk, maybe at seven, and one of him in my father's arms on the benches in front of Playland a year earlier are special treasures. It may no longer be, but then it was a careless beach town, particularly at the end near Playland, that hadn't seemed to change or care about changing in all the years we vacationed there. And I can see Lucas, his hair blown back by the wind, on those rides.

As I read of your bargains with God, I thought of myself. Every day, I ask God to let me take Wade's place. And failing that, to hold my boy as I would hold him, to protect him from our grief, to give him every happiness to which a child of his righteousness would be entitled, and to let him experience ecstasy. I ask for John's health, and for Cate's health, safety and happiness. And I ask God to give me faith.

It is unfair—how often that word is right— that there should be only six years of memories of Lucas. How comforting that those six are so deeply embroidered. How privileged I am that you have shared that with us.

I was privileged to be with Gordon and later Phil and Shelby and Astrid and Sue and Michael, and with their children or with their memories of their children. So often they said what I wished I had had the words to say, but it was more than that.

So many days I felt as if I had fallen into a deep black
hole, unable even to know which way was up anymore. These people—and too many others to name—
reached their hands out of the darkness and drew
me to a ledge where I could get my footing again. I
would fall and they would reach. They would fall
and I would reach. They sent me poems when I
needed poems and hugs when I needed hugs.

And sometimes in the midst of the advice and
the imaginary hugs were new maps we might follow, like the one offered by Skip Smeiska.

Skip's son Joshua died in September after Wade.
Josh, who was idolized by his younger brother
Matthew, was nearly nineteen when he died. It is
not unusual for teen grief to be expressed as anger
or hostility, but when seventeen-year-old Matthew
closed up altogether, Skip became concerned and
wrote Matthew a letter. What looked like a Christmas letter to a son was much more. Skip wrote to
Matthew, but I heard it, too. Skip's story is a road
map, really.

An artist who was successful in many medi-
ums—ink, oil, watercolor—wanted desperately
to be an accomplished woodworker, a carpenter.

He tried—small items, mostly, wooden bowls and platters, a breadbox, even a chain—but he was never satisfied. One day, the artist's wife asked him to make a table. Not only would he be working in wood, he would be responding to a request from the wife he dearly loved. He worked long and hard and produced for her a table, plain and solid and strong, not unlike the artist himself. The table became a part of their household. His family gathered there for supper. There they played games together. His children did their homework at his plain table, and there he wrote letters to friends and his wife made cookies. The table was as solid as his family.

One night a thief broke in. For some reason that would never make sense to anyone, he stole one of the legs to the table. The artist and his family were sad. How could they ever use this beloved table again if it only had three legs? But it was the only table they had, so they tried. Every time they tried to use the table, though, any item near where the leg had been went crashing to the floor, upsetting the table and the family. They tried putting heavy items on the opposite corner of the table to balance it, but the heavy items took so much of the table that it was hard to use. Soon the leg below the corner where all the heavy items were started to move out and away from the other two legs. The table seemed doomed to collapse.

The artist, forlorn, took the table back to his workshop. He cut and carved, shaped and sanded until he had created from their sturdy four-legged table a slightly smaller but strong three-legged table. It was a work of art, unique, beautiful and functional. The artist became, as he worked, the fine carpenter he always wanted to be, and his family had their precious table back.

Our family is like that table. It was steady and strong, then for reasons we will never understand, we were robbed of one of our legs. We try to balance our table as it wobbles, we make an extra effort here or there to keep everything from crashing to the floor. But sometimes they come crashing anyway. We know our efforts are only good in the short run. In the long run, we have to remake, reshape our table. It won't be our old table, but we can, with faith and love, build from it a table that will stand.

Skip finished his message to Matthew "Merry Christmas, Son." But Skip had the good grace to post it to our whole Internet community, so his gift went to many more who were struggling, not just to Matthew.

I had tried to keep Wade alive. I had cobbled together a collection of ways to parent his memory, to introduce him to others, to keep him as a part of the lives of those who loved him when he lived and breathed. I had, in effect, moved the heavy objects to the table so that it would not come crashing down, so that the old table could be central to my life, just as the boy had been central.

It did not happen on the day I read Skip's story. It happened slowly as I began to accept what I could not change and started to create my new life as the mother of Cate and then Emma Claire and Jack and, separately and differently, the bereaved mother of Wade. He is no less dear to me, but the longer I held him in this limbo between having died and whatever it was I craved, the longer I was in limbo, too. I admit, it still makes me cry to type the words "Wade is dead." I still see, when I allow myself, the tenderness that crossed over his face when he would look at me or the way he would reach, almost secretively, for his father's hand as they sat next to each other, or the way he would comfort and protect Cate, his arm over her shoulder, bending down and whispering in her ear. I don't have to bury the memory to accept that I have buried the boy.

Having the opportunity in a safe place to say what I needed to say about my boy and about my pain allowed me to move forward. Parenting his memory at his grave and at the places we have created because of him—the Learning Labs (there is now a second in Goldsboro), the high school short-story contest, even the garden at his grave—I could express my need always to be his mother. Finding in the ashes something to save, something worthwhile to parent, has made each day without his physical presence less painful.

And recognizing that if I buried myself in his death, I was leaving, as part of his legacy, a wreck of a human unable to do what he would have wanted me to do: be a mother to his beloved sister. More than that, too. Wade's life would cease to exist. The way he cared for those around him—never sending anyone away, sitting with the outcast at lunch, intervening when classmates harassed another student—that would be gone. All he valued and all he loved would not matter. All that would matter was that he was dead. Wade would be his death and not his life. Picking up the phone and making plans for lunch, buying a new dress, and going to a basketball game all sound like such little things, but they were a very big step for me.

The biggest step was having more children. Wade died in April of 1996. Emma Claire was born in April of 1998, and Jack was born in May of 2000. It was a conscious decision to have more children. What, John and I wondered in our quiet house in Raleigh, will ever bring happiness back into the house in which Cate will live? What brings us joy? The answer was clear: children. Although my great-grandmother had had a child at fifty years old without medicines, I didn't count on genetic good fortune. We went to the doctor and I started a regimen of shots and medicines to increase the likelihood that we would have children. I was forty-eight when I had Emma Claire, and—with my AARP card in hand—I was fifty when I had Jack a month before Cate graduated from high school. If Cate was my someone "for whom to remain," as Mark Helprin put it, I now had two more someones for whom to live. And to whom I could introduce their brother.

We wonder, sometimes, how it is that our son is so different from our daughter, or our oldest is so different from his younger brother. They were born into the same family, we say; how could they be so different? Well, the truth is that they were not born into the same family. Wade was born to two parents who had no other children. And Cate was born into a family of three. She did not know the family he knew. Emma Claire and Jack were born into yet other families, and their families included a brother who had died before their birth. That is completely different from Wade's family. As the parents, it seems like the same family changing and growing—and sometimes sadly contracting. But for me, I had to accept that I no longer had Wade's family. I had the family of our last child; I had Jack's. But Jack's and Emma Claire's families definitely include Wade.

I was working one afternoon when Emma Claire came in with a picture of Wade in her hand. "It makes me sad," she said. I thought I knew what she was thinking, but I did not. "It makes me sad that Jack never got to know Wade." Emma Claire had heard so much about her older brother that she didn't realize that she never knew him when he was alive. What to say? All I said was "It makes me sad, too."

But in truth it made me happy, too. After we are gone, we fade a little with the death of each person who knew us. Who is left to say our name or remember some moment we treasure? Who, we ask, are those people in the picture in front of grandmother's house? And here were two more people—quite young people; Jack was born twenty-one years after Wade was born—who would remember Wade, and remember him not just as he was when he died, but how he was as a boy and what he wrote when he was seven as well as what he wrote when he was fifteen.

❧

It was less than a year before Wade died when he and I sat in the family room looking at picture albums. We were looking at a photograph of him standing on the back stoop, his knit shirt tucked into khaki shorts, an enormous smile revealing a missing tooth, and a big sticker on his shirt with his name. His first day of kindergarten.

"I miss that boy," I said to Wade.

"I am right here," he answered.

"Oh, I love the boy who is right here, but that boy, that little boy is gone. I have the big you, but I no longer have that little boy and I miss him," I said, giving the Wade beside me a hug.

Understanding that he was gone and I was never getting him back was so much easier to accept when I had lost the little Wade but still had the big Wade. Now, with empty arms, I miss them both.

CHAPTER 6

Eternity

*O*thers have faced each of the struggles I have
faced, and many have faced much deeper chasms.
In each challenge, I have met people of enormous
faith for whom that faith was what they needed to
be resilient, to find in each challenge the love of
their god. It is a great blessing, and in the many moments when I have not found the solace I need in
faith alone, I have been envious of their peace and
the grace in which they stand. The problem of how
to view death was the biggest cloud that stood between me and my faith. The faithful were lucky and
knew and believed in something that gave them
peace. But to some who wanted to hold on to their
faith and could not, who wanted the peace now denied them, James Russell Lowell wrote the anthem:

. . .

Your logic, my friend, is perfect,

Your moral most drearily true;
But, since the earth clashed on her coffin,
I keep hearing that, and not you.

Console if you will, I can bear it;
'Tis a well-meant alms of breath;
But not all the preaching since Adam
Has made Death other than Death.
. . .
That little shoe in the corner,
So worn and wrinkled and brown,
With its emptiness confutes you,
And argues your wisdom down.

I knew if I could believe in the deepest part of me that death was more than just death, if I could have but the hope of one day with my son, I could live through the other days knowing I had that one I could share with him. And if I could embrace that we could have—together—life after death reunited, I could live with such peace now, knowing I would be with him—not in a year, but someday. But belief in that required belief in a place where we would reunite, a heaven, and therefore a god. But what kind of God could there be if He allowed the wind

to take Wade from us? Could I expect such benefi-
cence from the God who let him die?

In the Book of Job, chapter 1, verses 18 and 19,
a messenger comes to Job and says, "Thy sons and
thy daughters were eating and drinking in the el-
dest brother's house, and, behold, there came a great
wind from the wilderness, and smote the four corners of the house, and it fell upon the young men
and they are dead." Wade was driving to the beach
when he died. The invisible wind crossed the eastern North Carolina fields and pushed his car off the
road, and he could not right it and it flipped and,
crushed, it fell in upon Wade, and he died. The invisible wind. The hand of God? The hand of Satan
that God had loosened on Job? Is his death a response to his or our failings, or is it a test of God?
How can I lean on a God who had taken this righteous boy, or even on one who had allowed him to
be taken? The faith that might have been so important to me was, I will be honest, more than sorely
tested. I had to reconcile what I had believed with
what I had experienced. I had believed in a God
who protected the righteous; God's punishment is
meted out to those who have sinned. What's more, I
had believed that God would intervene to protect

the innocent. How, at forty-six, having seen what I had of the world, having walked around the site of the children's hospital at Hiroshima, near the epicenter of the atomic bomb, having seen injustice and misery reposed among the innocent across the globe, I still believed this, I cannot say. I only know that I did, until April 4, 1996.

I wrote, after Wade died, trying to sort it out: "I haven't the will to be angry with God. I don't understand, and all my efforts at understanding are thwarted, paths into brambles, paths into deserts. And yet, I cannot be angry. I know I want something of God. I want to be beside my son, and if I am to hope for this, He is my only way. Where would anger bring me? Further and farther from my boy? What use is that, save the satisfaction of it? The only satisfaction I crave is the warmth of my boy's touch and the sound of his voice. I need that hope. It sustains me." But the search for hope was hard, and that path to God's grace was difficult to find. The map I knew did not comport with the ground on which I was walking.

The God to whom I prayed daily for Wade's eternal soul had to be another god than the one I had imagined. I had to reconsider what I had been taught. My God, my new understanding of God is that he does not promise us protection and intervention. He promises only salvation and enlightenment. This is our world, a gift from God, and we make it what it is. If it is unjust, we have made it so. If there is boundless misery, we have permitted it. If there is suffering, it came from man's own action or inaction. Abel killed Cain; God did not. Wade's death didn't belong to God. It belonged to this earth. I could still pray for Wade's eternal soul because I no longer had to blame that same God to whom I prayed unsuccessfully for his return to life.

The journey to my new understanding of God made me also understand and sympathize with the doubt of others. And among those who grieved, at my face-to-face grief groups and particularly on the Internet, doubt was a well-known companion. So many of us grew up in religious households or found the society around us organized along certain religious assumptions that few of us came to death entirely from an atheistic or agnostic position. When death or disease struck those we loved, we looked for something to make it make sense, even to make it not really so. We prayed that diseases would be cured and bones healed. We looked to religion; it is where we were taught to look; it is where our faith drove us. Our death rituals are built around religion; our funerals are largely in places of worship; the headstones near our loved ones espouse it. So here we were, grappling with God. Some good and righteous mourners found what was needed; some good and righteous mourners did not.

Part of the appeal of religion, viewed dispassionately (which is not, I know, the right or proper way to consider faith, and I mean no disparagement whatever by it), is that religion provides a way to believe that our loved ones have not really died. Their bodies have died, their spirit lives. The thought is more than comforting. Not only have they not ceased to exist, reunion is possible. Where does the atheist or the agnostic go for that same degree of comfort? There is no place, for I do not think there is the same degree of comfort elsewhere. I do think there are things one can do to help the spirit of those whom we love live on after their deaths, ways in which we can translate their spirit into tangible things or activities that represent their spirit. We can build statues, and we do. We can write books, and we do. We can find ways in which we can translate what is temporal—life on earth—into something permanent. None of these require faith. And the permanence they provide is real. How many religions have come and gone or changed since Ovid wrote *Metamorphoses,* in which he described the endurance of literature in the epilogue?

> *Now I have done my work. It will endure,*
> *I trust, beyond Jove's anger, fire, and sword,*
> *Beyond time's hunger. The day will come, I know,*
> *So let it come, that day which has no power*
> *Save over my body, to end my span of life*
> *Whatever it may be. Still, part of me,*
> *The better part, immortal will be borne*
> *Above the stars; . . .*
> *I shall be read, and through all centuries,*
> *If prophecies of bards are ever truthful,*
> *I shall be living, always.*

And I am reading the words, so maybe Ovid is right. And then again, he is not living; the making of statues, the writing of words are not the answer I need, however comforting they are in the here and now, because the existence of other roads to an enduring presence, to "living, always" does not, unfortunately, diminish the need for a spiritual answer.

What I needed was not Wade's eternal memory; I needed his eternal life, a life greater than sixteen short years, and I needed the hope of reunion.

Until my own heart could settle on a way to make life and death and hope as much a part of our being as breath, the platitudes and parables, religious or not, did not help me. So I read, and I prayed for my son's eternal protection and for faith for myself to believe in that protection. And I prayed for answers, answers that my faith would never provide. Faith would one day provide a credo for the rest of life without my child, but like the statues and poems and physical memorials, it could not answer the question I ask every day after a loss or an injustice or any suffering: It cannot tell me why.

How rare it must be for someone to say, "I deserve this cancer; it is a proper punishment for my sins," or even more unlikely, "God was right to take my child, for I am not pious." We all have to redraw lines and rearrange our expectations of faith in these moments, and it is understandable that we do not come to rest with precisely the same understanding. In my online grief groups, there were Christians and Jews and Muslims and Buddhists, and there were many with no faith at all. We had talked about graves and headstones and cremation and every manner of thing, and so we felt secure enough in this group to talk about this, the most important of things, the likelihood of eternal life and ultimate reunion. But those who needed, understandably, to believe that eternal life was absolutely assured perhaps by some ritual in which their child had engaged surely hurt, by their strident insistence on the importance of these rituals, those whose children did not so confirm their faith. So arguments began among people who had previously understood the rules of the group to be that we would, at all costs, protect one another. I had to wonder, as it happened, what God, looking down on His creation, would think of us. He would, I imagined, be perplexed that we understood so little of what He wanted from us.

But now it was more about what we wanted from Him.

If you are able, like Job, to place yourself firmly in the hands of your god, you have, in my view, a greater gift than resilience. You do not have to come to terms with a new reality of a child in a grave or with a disease silently ravaging your body. This is not a new reality; this is what your god has ordained for you, handing you the suffering in one hand and the faith with which to come to terms with it in the other. Some who are not fully satisfied with God's arms or God's answers looked elsewhere. I will not judge them, for what they got is what they needed. I wanted a god, but I needed a different understanding of my God than the one in which I had believed before the wind swept Wade from the road.

I listened as there were discussions of mysticism and after-death communications and other places I was not willing to go. I would not then and do not now condemn that search. What do we know, really? We are all on a journey to understanding, and we cannot know the end or scope of it, and even in the most mundane ways, we can hardly come close. I was—and still am—completely amazed by telephones: that I might dial a set of digits here in North Carolina, and my sister might answer the telephone more than a thousand miles away in Florida, and that I speak and she recognizes my voice. What happened to my voice? It must have been taken apart and sent in waves to the sky and back to someplace on earth where it knew it was meant for her and was sent only to her, and the voice that was waves was put back together and became again a voice, incredibly, that she could recognize. And what is more, we can talk, even talk right over one another, so it seems all the taking apart and sending and putting back together happens at once. I remember talking to my father overseas one time when I was a girl. His voice was almost his voice, but it would crackle and fall apart, and there would be pauses, the last words echoing while I waited my turn to speak back. I know that the old almost-voices and the new perfect-voices are only physics, but it is a wonder. A wonder that seemed like a trick, then seemed imperfect, and then became what we know and accept: That is my sister's voice, and this is mine. What other rough edges and crackles will we smooth so that what seems a difficult or impossible communication—even communication across the barrier of life—is clear, is commonplace? About much more important things, I am not vain enough to think I know at all. You do not have to believe in order to believe that you do not know.

We came to understand doubt expressed rawly or expressed in searches for answers elsewhere as but a search for meaning, reassurance, hope. We came to understand that religious vehicles that had for millennia encapsulated our spiritual expectations may, nonetheless, be insufficient for some to explain the terrible briefness of the life of one child. We tried to make life and death, and hope, as much a part of our beings as the air we breathed at their graves, and until we managed that, the platitudes and parables of others were meaningless. So we read, and we prayed, and, frankly, many of us wandered. And wondered. I still wonder what it was I was looking forward to. I wanted to embrace the image of some eternity, but I could not quite make it form. What was the heaven for which I pined? There, if I longed to touch him, would I feel his cheek? Or would I simply be freed of my longing to feel his cheek?

As I have felt further, less devastating blows in the years after Wade's death, I cannot understand how I merited these blows. What did I do? Even though I think I know better, I still continue to ask and I continue to wonder. And then I remind myself: This is the world we made; its flaws are our flaws; its shortcomings are our shortcomings; and the degree to which there is injustice or unprovoked suffering is just a reflection of our failures. But because, in order to reach this point, I have to accept a

God who does not intervene, I have to accept that I cannot expect intervention now. I do not pray for my health. God gave me this world, and He gave me free will. It is my world, and now, if I am able, I have to fix it.

CHAPTER 7

2007

*A*nother city, another town hall, another morning shower. The moments that will change our lives are often not in the monumental events writ large on our calendars. My husband was running for vice president of the United States, and certainly the next monumental moment in our lives would be on November 3, 2004, election day. But sometimes the critical moments are hidden in an ordinary day. My life changed on October 21 as I showered. Standing in a hotel bathroom in Kenosha, Wisconsin, I felt a lump, flat and smooth, like a slice of plum midway between my armpit and nipple. I convinced myself that it was just a cyst. Allowing myself to think that it could be a cyst allowed me to dress that day, to lead the town hall, and then to campaign for another week before a mammogram and ultrasound took away such foolish illusions. Maybe not so foolish: No women in my family had had breast cancer save my father's sister. On my mother's side, the side important for breast cancer, I thought, there was nothing. And this was, I believed, nothing but a cyst. Since it was the size of a generous slice of plum, though, I would have it checked when I could. But it was eleven days before election day, and I had a full schedule. I couldn't get it checked for a few days without canceling events and alerting the press. And I couldn't tell the press because they would say the threat of cancer was a play for sympathy, and I didn't tell John because these days leading up to the election might be the most life-changing days of his life, and my plum shouldn't be on his mind unless it needed to be. So far, it was just a cyst-plum, and it didn't need to be.

A week later, after a secret mammogram and biopsy while I was home in Raleigh to vote early, it was clear it was not just a cyst. Watching the radiologist read the ultrasound monitor, I knew it could not be something benign like a cyst. The plum was likely to be cancer, and I had to tell John. He jumped into action. He arranged for a biopsy in Boston the day after the election, and we barreled through the final days of the campaign as if that sword were not dangling over our heads. In truth, the campaign

gave us each a respite from letting ourselves go
where we knew we would likely have to go after
the biopsy the next week: The test was likely to confirm I had cancer, we were certain. And a week
later, the day after the 2004 presidential election that
did not alter John's life (or mine) in any significant
way, we drove from somber words of the concession
speeches at Faneuil Hall in Boston to Massachusetts
General Hospital and the somber words we knew
were coming.

I cannot tell you whether knowing the words
"you have cancer" are coming makes it easier, since
I did not get to do it two ways. I did it one way, and
although that was bad enough, I suspect that it was
easier getting used to the idea of cancer over a period of a couple of weeks, getting a chance to tell my
family in little pieces rather than having to hear it
one day and having everyone sitting at my knees in
tears all at once after that. So my husband, my oldest daughter and I stood erect and took with resignation the words: *You have cancer.* It had been a
life-changing day after all. We would have to adjust
our lives to the disease.

At first it was not cancer itself to which I adjusted but the idea of cancer. The disease was inside

me, but except for that plum, there would be no reason to suspect it was there based on how I felt or how I looked. Even when I started to look like a cancer patient in external ways and to feel in internal ways like I was sick, it was, honestly, the medicine I was taking to stop the cancer, not the plum-sized tumor itself, that was responsible. If the pharmacist who was preparing my chemotherapy infusion happened to drop a bag of my medicine on the floor, he would wear protective gear to clean it up; it was sufficiently toxic to require that degree of precaution. And yet we pumped it directly into my veins for several hours every two weeks. It was no wonder I was feeling lousy.

In those months, that first year when the chief nurse Ann was greeting me at the hospital door, when Dr. Warren was measuring the shrinking tumor, when my infusion nurse Mercedes was making that dreadful medicine seem tolerable, I never believed I would die from this disease. I certainly did not want breast cancer, but as diseases go breast cancer—when contained in my breast—was unlikely to kill me. This would be an obstacle in my story, an obstacle that would be hard to hurdle but one that would not change my course. Even if it was not easy, I could do it, knowing I would not have to accept a whole new life again. And when I had breast cancer in 2004 and 2005, it was just plain physically hard. It does not matter whether it was the idea of the disease or the reality of the medicine that made those months hard. My joints ached, every one of them. Depending on when it was in my chemotherapy cycle, I wouldn't want anything to eat or I would stand in front of the refrigerator famished. I would tire in a morning of meetings. My eyesight worsened. I felt empty-headed; I would look for a word and I could not find it; I would start a sentence and forget where I was headed. All of these limitations were good only for my younger children, then four and six, because child's play was the easiest activity to handle. I could play Chutes and Ladders for hours . . . as long as I was prone. I could read the large print of children's books. And when I was not sleeping or playing with the children, when I was not trying to write thank-you notes to well-wishers or attending a meeting about what came next for us, it was mostly sports on television. After two years of campaigning that kept me from watching sports, it was now ESPN all the time. I missed the 2004 Olympics, but it was the

NFL playoffs and then the college bowl games and, taking me through the end of chemotherapy and recovery from my surgery, it was college basketball and spring baseball in the majors.

So I watched television and read aloud to the children and read an astounding 65,000 e-mails that were sent to me. In the months that followed, I would also read 30,000 pieces of regular mail, some on homemade cards, some with gifts included. It might seem, given the numbers, that I would tire of reading them, but I did not. Each was a personal gift, packaged in a way that reflected the giver, letting me imagine them placing a cap they had knitted into a box or letting the youngest child in the family who had signed a card reach up to the post box to mail their card. For years John and I have played a game with the children in the car. When it is your turn, you choose a house you are passing and you make up a story about the people in the house. A well-kept garden or dead flowers in a window box; clothes hanging on the line; children's toys in the yard; an empty horse-trailer; all the details of life that give us clues about the people for whom that is home. You have to notice as many details as possible in the time it takes to pass the house. You then make up an elaborate story about the house and its inhabitants, filling in the spaces between the details with which you have been provided. A house with a newly constructed ramp was a soldier returning from battle; the now-untended vegetable garden the result of his wife's caring for him instead of it. I was doing that for the cards, e-mails, and gifts and their senders. It made it seem more like they were people I knew than the strangers almost every one of them really was. Sometimes on the cards or letters they would give me an outline to fill in; they would tell me about themselves: They had had breast cancer, they were a Republican, they had lost a child, their father had been in the military too. For quite a while, I was never lonely. My living room was filled with good-hearted strangers.

Ensconced on the couch with prayer quilts they had sent tucked around me and my latest favorite knit cap over my head, I wondered how other women, less comforted, made it through these painful months. Well, for most, of course, the months were not as empty as mine. Many had to go back to work, achy and tired or not. I was lucky—I did not. Single mothers might not be able to rely on their children's father to take care of the children; I was lucky—after the election John was able to devote himself to me and the children. A stranger who had read of another woman's cancer was not sending them a prayer quilt or a get-well card. I was lucky— someone somewhere was thinking of me, praying for me. I sat reading their letters for hours, placing them back into boxes where they are still stored in my house. But I was lucky, too, in a frivolous way— how you simply spend these hours: I had young, resilient children, I had a husband who included me in his work, and I liked sports. So my days were filled with Chutes and Ladders and David Shannon's children's books, with meetings about what John was going to do now that the election was over (it turned out he started a poverty center in North Carolina), with my preliminary drawings of the house we would build when we returned home after my treatment, and with sports on television. Part of my recovery from this debilitating treatment was that I was busy in a fashion and I was not alone. But I cannot overestimate the importance of my belief that I would not die of this disease.

So many times between November 2004 and now I have sat in a hospital room, waiting for the doctor to come in and tell me what the latest scans tell her and what changes there have been in the previous three months. There are some of these potentially life-changing conversations, frankly, that melt together: the same doctor, the same room, the same report—no appreciable change, which meant I would not die of breast cancer. But the ones when the report is not the same? Those I never forget; they never melt into another day or into another season. Those I remember what I was wearing, the weather, the words the doctor used, where John and Cate sat. From that first tiny hospital room, crisp and spartan and white at Massachusetts General, where we first heard the word "cancer" spoken aloud to the basement room with a bed and a sink where John and I sat for hours waiting for the results of the bone scan and the CT, to the latest room in Chapel Hill in the old Gravely Building that has stood there since I was in college, where we heard that it was no longer contained and had spread to a couple of new places, the quiet life-changing moments grow to an imposing size.

There was a time, in 2005, when I was being treated for Stage 2 breast cancer and the news was almost always good. Doctors looking at ultrasound machines and smiling, a happy nurse handing me the gown into which I would change before the doctor came in, and finally the wave good-bye—the cancer was gone. Boy, it sounds so simple when months of basically happy reports fall over one another like that. Of course, the road to the smiles was more than bumpy. Like a Conestoga wagon crossing the far West, the whole of me shook for the entire ride—but now and again there was a beautiful sunset ahead that made it seem worth it and we were headed to good health again. The vision wasn't on the horizon, however; it was in a scan result or on an ultrasound screen or in the clean margins after the surgery. All beautiful, reassuring. I had determined not to let fear in, and it was easier when the reports all confirmed that I should not be afraid. But the reports only looked at my body that day; they could not see tomorrow.

My grandmothers each died in their nineties. I knew one of my great-grandmothers, who must have been nearly a hundred when she died. Until 2004, I believed I might live longer than all of them. I had been hospitalized to have children, but that was all. I took no medicines, prescription or otherwise. I was always dieting, but my blood pressure and my cholesterol were both low. Living to ninety-five seemed entirely possible. I had had children late in life, Emma Claire when I was forty-eight and Jack when I was fifty, so living a long life would mean that I would see them marry and I would live to hold their children. And now, suddenly, seeing even my oldest daughter, Cate, marry seems in jeopardy. In a moment—a "you have cancer" moment—all the genetic aces folded. I was—am—desperately afraid of losing the precious moments of life.

There were times even in those relatively optimistic early days, though, when I felt alone. There is part of this disease that belongs only to me. I never felt comfortable sharing the moments when logic left and the pain of the treatment magnified the risk of dying, when fear did come in. What could the people who love me do, anyway, I figured. It would only make them feel lousy that they could not honestly say anything that would change the reality I was facing. This is the catch-22: We protect them when they want and need to protect us, when they know we want and need protection. With each side protecting the other, neither of us gets what we want or need. But I always figured it was impossible to get what we needed. I had the disease, they could not change that. All I could do was guess what their reaction would be to my expression of my fears—impotence, I guessed—and what was the point of that? I kept from them my greatest fears precisely because they would respond with protestations that this was about tending to me, not about tending to them. And they, though they might keep a stiff upper lip with me, would, I discovered later, fall apart alone in fear and grief. They could not ask me to carry them through this. In our way of being gentle with each other, we never really see it from each other's perspective. I had to decide what I should share. My conclusion? I have shared very little. Maybe not talking about the fear was better anyway, not allowing it to own any more of me than it already did. And if it is not better, well, fortunately, we have more days to get it right.

In 2005, it seemed as if the cancer had been chased away. Maybe I had been right to deny fear a place in my life. Cancer was already scarring my body, taking my hair and my strength, taking a year of my life. I was right, I thought, not to hand it any more than it took by force. I still think that was right. But I was wrong and arrogant to think that I had somehow beaten back the disease.

In 2007, it was back. Spring was teasing us in Chapel Hill: The days were warm and bright, but by sunset winter reminded us that it was not quite done with us. And then it all seemed not to matter, except to think that the weather was mocking us. The cancer was back. Well, I suppose the doctors would say that it had never really gone. I thought I had chased it away with chemotherapy, with a surgery that left my breast disfigured, and with a month and a half of daily radiation two years before. But I had only chased away the big pieces; the smallest of pieces had stayed, hidden from scans, too small for imaging; they had stayed and then grown. And now here it was again, now grown, now in its new home. No longer in my breast, it had spread to my bones, maybe my lungs, maybe my liver. And it wasn't leaving. Not ever. In that moment, when I found out for certain that I would have cancer in me every single day until the one day it finally took my life, all the reasons to live and the reasons to die, the way to live if I could, all danced before me, twirling, enticing, until I chose a partner from among them. Live. Die. Fight. Curl up. Look for a hug. Give a hug. Cry. Cry. Cry.

Could there be a reason to die? "No" is the obvious answer, and it would be easy for me to say the conventional no, there is no reason to die. But if you had lost a child—as I had two weeks short of eleven years before I sat in that hospital room waiting for the results of the bone scans—you might see it a different way. Death looks different to someone who has placed a child in the ground. It is not as frightening. In fact, it is in some way buried deep within you almost a relief. The splendid author Mark Helprin wrote, in the introduction to *Almost Spring* by Gordon Livingston, "If you were on a ship battered by immense waves (and, believe me, you are) that swept your child from your arms would you not (given that you had no others for whom to remain) throw yourself into the deep, hoping for the chance that in the vast black ocean you might grab onto him? Comforted just to know that you would suffer the same fate? And if you had to remain, to protect others, would you not dream all your life of the day when, your responsibilities over, you would finally get to the sea?" It is not a death wish. It is an appreciation that there might be in death some relief that life itself could never offer.

But I did not want to dance with death.

What were the reasons to live? They lived and breathed before me. My children, the "others for whom to remain," certainly. I had buried Wade, but his sister Cate had just turned twenty-five, and, as strong as she was, I did not want her to test whether she was strong enough to lose any more of her family. Did Emma Claire, brilliant and fragile and kind, have the tools at eight years old to deal with cancer that I would surely have to tell her could take my life? And Jack, still six and precious and charmed— how hard would I have to make the news to break through his steadfast optimism? And Wade's death had reminded me what a gift life is, not to be taken for granted on a single day. I thought of the people who had written me in 2004—and many were writing again—who had said that you are alive today and that is a victory. The only answer was to live, as long and as well as I could. I determined, as I thought of them—and I recommit every time I look at them—to live long enough to die of something other than cancer. There is, I know, a continued arrogance in that.

My husband of almost thirty years sat next to me in a tiny basement examination room at the hospital as we got the news that the cancer had metastasized. The last three months had been hard. I had come to know his imperfections, and my sense of what our marriage meant, of who I was, of what was to happen to us and all we had done together, had been roiling in my head every minute of every day since. But here on this day, calm set in. John had been campaigning in Iowa as a candidate for the Democratic nomination for president, and, of course, he had come home for my tests, come home to the somber words of the doctor, come home to my frightened voice. It wasn't just that he was there—how could he not be?—it was the look of fear on his face. It was clear that through all that had happened, he never thought he would lose me. He counted, as I did, on the seemingly immutable fact that we had a profound and deep relationship that had withstood worse—the death of Wade—and that after that we had stood together and slept together and worked together.

His face now told me that he had never entertained the idea that I would not be a part of his life, even the center of his life, no matter what. He now knew to a certainty that I would die and he would live on without me and he was afraid. It was not yet clear whether I could forgive his transgression or whether I would continue to stand beside him, but that did not matter. None of that had anything to do with our prospects now as we sat in the hospital. What was clear was that I would not stand with him in all that life would send his way because cancer would take me at some point and he would be alone. The constancy of the love that had kept us together, had kept me with him, had been sorely tested, but now it was not what I would do faced with his indiscretion that mattered. Cancer was writing the script now. Cancer would decide. And, realizing this, he broke down with fear and love and regret. And once again I was the woman who had chosen him thirty years before and built a life and family with him. We were lovers, life companions, crusaders, side by side, for a vision of what the country could be, and we were an old married couple. At least for a while.

And that part about crusading together, it was the glue. Whatever might be ripping at our lives together, the cancer was stronger, but maybe the crusade was stronger too. And with the strength of these battles in which we were so clearly united, we would regain our strength. I grabbed hold of it. I needed to. I needed him to stand with me, and although I no longer knew what I could trust between the two of us, I knew I could trust in our work together. This was the life I had before the doctor's grim diagnosis. Is it so hard to understand that I so desperately wanted that life back, back before all the words and acts that might have separated us? I could not simply retreat to my home with nothing but death in my future. It might be hard to understand, but I had done nothing wrong at all, and yet my life, so carefully constructed, so carefully tended to, was being eaten away. What did I have to do to rescue it, to mend it back to how I wanted it to be? I got some hints as we waited.

The words of the nurse who was putting in an IV line about John's dedication to health care, the holding-my-breath looks of the others who were awaiting scan results and the smiles they broke into as John pushed my wheelchair by them, the memories of tested but hopeful faces I had seen for the last five years as I crossed the country, I grabbed on to all of them. I could do this. I would do this. I found a dance partner, one that allowed me to dance with a husband who had disappointed me and one that allowed me to dance for my children——a dance of an intact family fighting for causes more important than any one of us. It had been part of our wedding vows thirty years earlier in a country church not two miles from our home today—to work for a more just world—and John asked if we could renew those vows that summer when we had our thirtieth anniversary. I could do this. I would show my dear children that I was alive and that it really only matters how we handle our worst moments, and see what Mother is doing? See how Daddy is helping?

In the next hours, we sat with our closest staff—all friends for years, soldiers in the same war—and we told them, their eyes filled with tears, that the cancer had metastasized but we would continue to campaign. John's indiscretion seemed a million miles away; I cannot say I even thought of it. I thought only of the bright spots on the bone scan, in my hip and on my ribs, and of my doctor's conclusion that it was not good but also not dire. We hugged everyone and smiled and planned for tomorrow.

And writing this, it seems so simple. All the fear seems to be but a setting for some larger battles yet to be waged. And yet in the moment, the pain and the fear were real, overshadowing, dark, and I had to find a partner bigger and stronger and more important than my own cancer. I was lucky, for I had been dancing with that partner for years.

We chose to announce the metastasized cancer publicly—although I did not know with any real certainty what my prognosis was—and to continue with my husband's political campaign—although I did not know the prognosis for the campaign, either. I only knew that both were alive that day and that all I could do was to make today count. I did the only thing I knew to do: I pressed on with what still seemed important to me. It probably doesn't matter so much what those things are. What mattered, in order to put one foot in front of another, was that there was some reason to do that, some reason to get up and shower, some reason to make what remained of my hair look reasonable, some reason to, well, live even though the hand life had dealt looked increasingly bleak, increasingly lonely.

I am guessing that I am not the only cancer patient who does not talk about fear. Or who doesn't know what to do with talk of anything more than a year away. Does it matter where the Olympics are held in eight years? Maybe not for me. So when there is such talk, my mind immediately wanders:

How long will I have been dead by then? And just as quickly I push such thoughts away. Part of resisting the disease is captured in simply not letting the fear of tomorrow control the quality of today. The Rodgers and Hammerstein song from *The King and I* makes the point better than I can: I whistle a happy tune, and every single time, the happiness in the tune convinces me that I'm not afraid. Powering through the fear may seem like denial, but fear doesn't change the prognosis. It only changes the way I would feel between now and whenever the inevitable occurs. So that is what I did. And it worked, at least at first.

When I watched my father die in 2008, I looked at a body too weak to fight any longer, his skin smooth and milky and thin, his eyes with a film over them separating his world from ours. "You can go if you want," I told him when we were alone before the others gathered, "but if you can, wait for everyone to get here. Then you can choose." And he did hold on, he held to the tiniest thread of life until his family gathered in yet another hospital room and until each of us said what we needed to say, until we all laughed about his years of foolishness and cried about his years of foolishness, until we sang to him and read to him and held his hand.

Until we knew it was time to stop. The nurses turned off the machines that warned us how close he was to death, and we waited together quietly, reverently, until the green line on the one remaining muted monitor went silently flat. His sister didn't know when it happened, my mother no longer understood even that he had died. But he did know; someplace in him he knew, and I can almost imagine the wink he would have given if he could as he slipped out the door, leaving the rest of us, the living, alone.

And that is as good as it gets.

Like the rest of us—for we are all dying—I am dying. I haven't any idea how long it will take for the cancer now metastasized at least to my bones to strangle life from me; I haven't any notion of whether the medicine I take today will stave it off for another month or another year, and I do not know what comes next when this medicine starts losing its battle with the cancer cells.

And it teases me—or I tease myself with the fear of it. I was traveling in 2007 when I felt a rough spot on the back of my neck. No matter how I turned the single hotel mirror, it would not reveal the mark I was feeling. When I came home, I checked. It was long and brownish and rough. Had the cancer metastasized to the skin? Was that even possible? I did what I promised myself I would never do: I googled "skin cancer" and sat at my computer with two mirrors and a screen full of images. As I compared them, Cate walked in. She looked at the screen and in a cautious tone she asked, "What are you doing, Mom?" I tried to sound nonchalant: "Oh, I felt this rough spot on my neck," flicking my hand over the spot in as carefree a way as I could manage. "Just checking on what it might be." She looked at the images on the screen, and she looked at the place on my neck. Then, turning to leave, she said with real nonchalance, "I don't know what skin cancer looks like, but I do know what a curling iron burn looks like." Two nights of going to sleep rubbing the place on my neck, measuring the feel of it, and it was a curling iron burn. Death averted, or just stupid fear? Stupid, mind-numbing, all-encompassing fear.

Sometimes the fear is justified. As I was writing this book, through the fall of 2008, I felt a pain in my back. It would come and go, but I am prone to move things that are too heavy or to lift a child I should not, and I let myself believe that was all there was to it. Just as I had done when I found the plum that must be a cyst in my breast three years earlier. When I go every two weeks to the hospital for my chemotherapy infusion, I see Jerome. He is gentle and patient, a beekeeper by avocation, which seems perfect to me somehow—coming close to what could hurt him but never getting hurt because of that gentility. Jerome would ask me as he took my blood pressure and prepared my biweekly IV infusion whether I had any new pains. "Some back pain," I would answer, and he would write it down. Jerome would tell Dr. Carey, and Dr. Carey would tell me if it required any special attention, so I could forget about it. Until the next pain. But as Christmas approached, the pain became more frequent, and I could pinpoint where on a rib in my back it was centered. Again I did what I no longer bother telling myself not to do: I googled "bone cancer and symptoms." The intermittent pain was there on the list of symptoms, in words I might have written to describe my pain. We moved up the scheduled MRI.

First a lovely technician did an X-ray. Maybe the rib had fractured. I was now praying for a fracture. I lay on the table as she prepared for the X-ray. She maneuvered the machinery over my pelvis. It is my rib, I said. I don't have an order for an X-ray of your rib; I only have an order for your pelvis. I started to cry. I don't think until that moment I recognized how afraid I was. Her young voice became maternal and comforting. She would take care of it. A few phone calls later, she was taking X-rays of my ribs. Dr. Carey's nurse Leslie called: There was no fracture. The next morning I would have an MRI, and the following day I would meet with Dr. Carey.

Cate was home for Christmas, so she, John, and I sat in yet another hospital room waiting for the MRI results. On other days, Dr. Carey would come in and her first words would be: *You are fine.* She did not start that way. This time, the already metastasized cancer had spread. A couple of places were slightly larger and there were two new sites. She said the words softly, serenely, alternating looking at me and at the report in her hand. There was, however she tempered the results, only a minimal rise in the tumor markers in my blood tests.

I didn't hear the words "minimal rise." I still don't hear it. All I heard is that the cancer is growing again. I had expected to hear it, but that didn't help. I had felt it, I had looked it up. It could only be one thing, really, and yet hearing the words was so much worse than I had thought it would be. My chest felt tight and it felt like blood was rushing to my forehead, pushing at the backs of my eyes. The Christmas tree was up at home; half the presents were wrapped; the kitchen counters were covered in cookies and pies. But that last Christmas—was it this one?—was just that much closer. I would like to say how brave and stiff-lipped I was, but that would be a lie. None of us were, really. Cate sat perfectly still, her hand on top of mine, watching first Dr. Carey and then me. John leaned against the wall and could not look at me at first. When he did, I could see that he had his own version of pain and fear. We listened, agitated, near tears. What are the options? She suggested one. One? Is there only one?

I am now back on a medicine that I had been on before when the cancer had not spread. I had been on it for about nine months after the metastasis was first diagnosed. The same medicine? Was that it? I wondered. Should I have never gone off? Should I have insisted that the side effects, stiff dry hands and feet, were fine? Should I not even have reported them? I could second-guess myself, but what did I know, really? I depended on Dr. Carey, and she seemed calm. I tried to steal some of her serenity for myself, but I could not. I was panicked, and I was angry, too. Off one drug, then back on the same drug? Wasn't there supposed to be an arsenal? Where is the arsenal? I wanted to know. At the first sign of the metastasis in 2007, we were told there would be an arsenal—one drug works until it doesn't work anymore and then we go to the next drug, and all the time I am taking the next drug, researchers are working on the one that will follow that. An ever-growing arsenal. One and then the next. But I was simply going back to what I had taken before. I had depended on that arsenal.

If this doesn't work, will there even be another drug? I asked Dr. Carey. Will it work? I asked myself. At home, I stand up and I feel a pinch in my leg and I cannot move it, and I wonder: Is this it? Is this the beginning of it? Each ache, each pain, each mark is a reminder: Death is inside me, waiting patiently, and it, not I, will decide when an ache is more than an ache. And that is my new reality. I wanted to grab hold of my old life, like the warrior's wife with her new changed husband, new changed reality fighting for what used to be. But my old life was gone. I had no idea how much of this new life I had. As I had traveled, generous warm people had told me of their aunt or a colleague who had lived twenty years, twenty-five years after metastasis. Their good fortune had been a four-leaf clover I kept in my pocket. It had happened to them; it could happen to me. But I wasn't feeling particularly lucky anymore.

I knew that I have to get ready to die. There still is no prognosis on which I can rely. If I had a timeline, it would make every decision so much easier. I do not want to plan to die. All I know is that it will be at my door more quickly than I want. I don't think, as it comes, I will have my father's grace. Now, despite my words that I have a reason why death would not be so terrible, I want to live. I admit that I spend a great deal of time pretending that I would be fantastically lucky to live a decade, that I would be happy to have another decade when I know I want much more. But just as there is more than a decade, there is also less. There are moments when I believe death is only a whisper away. I try to get the teeter-totter to balance somewhere in the middle; it is rarely possible. When my mind teeters to death, I push off as hard as I can, trying to land on life. Mostly I can do that.

It does not do me much good to talk about it, to spend some of my living time planning to die, giving more of me to the disease than it will ultimately demand. But I cannot pretend I didn't wish I knew. I cannot pretend that I didn't wish the disease was in my control. All that is in my control is how I live now. I could fill the days with fears—there are plenty of those—or I could fill them with the best joys I can cobble together. My husband wrote, in his book *Four Trials*—in part, I admit, on my recommendation, "I have learned two great lessons—that there will always be heartache and struggle, and that people of strong will can make a difference. One is a sad lesson, the other is inspiring. I choose to be inspired." There is enough unhappiness and pain to fill my days, but I choose to be happy.

Until I know—and the only things I can really know are that researchers have found a cure or that my death is imminent—I fill my days with things that matter to me and I find comfort where I can with those who have loved me perfectly or imperfectly. In 2004 when my cancer was first reported, I turned, as I often have, to the Internet for support and comfort. There, on Democratic Underground, I read a comment someone had posted under a thread offering me support. The comment included lines from a Leonard Cohen song, "Anthem":

Ring the bells that still can ring.
Forget your perfect offering.
There is a crack in everything.
That's how the light gets in.

It has become my anthem. I did something unlike me: I had the words placed on the wall high in my kitchen, a reminder that the pain, the loneliness, the fear are all part of the living. There is no such thing as perfection, and we have a choice about how we integrate the imperfect into our lives.

The idea that we—even, maybe particularly, those of us in the public eye—lead some sort of charmed and perfect lives is, sadly, so far from the truth. Everything in the fish-eye lens we have of our own lives is distorted, and as that lens moves across our stories, different threats loom large, outsized by the public view, dwarfing all the pieces so perfectly placed for that perfect life. The trick, I suppose, in a public or a private life is to recognize that the outsized monsters are distortions and that in real life the ground and the sky are in the right place and the foundations that we built are, likely, still standing. I was testing that, surely, but I was determined to adapt to the distortions.

Perhaps it was 1998 when Roger Elliot, our min-
ister at Edenton Street United Methodist Church in
Raleigh, gave a sermon in which he talked about a
congregant who had called him. I am overwhelmed,
the man had said, and I need to see you. Roger, of
course, saw him and listened as the man complained
of all that was wrong with his life, financially, spiri-
tually, personally. He felt as we all often feel: help-
less against high odds, alone and without options.
The man volunteered that he felt like Phil Connors,
the weatherman played by the brilliant comedic
actor Bill Murray, who wakes up every morning and
it is, again, Groundhog Day. I am like Phil Connors, he said; every day is the same miserable day
over and over with no hope of that ever changing. I
think he must have left before the end of the film.
Phil Connors was wretched, certainly, and every
day—especially the exact same every day—was undeniably lousy. Phil didn't even stop to think about
what he wanted; he, like the congregant, just complained. He almost basked in and definitely reflected
the misery of a life symbolized by the banality of
grown men waiting in a cold rain for a groundhog
to appear. Phil was nowhere and going nowhere,
just as the congregant felt was true of his own life,

and they each had fallen into a reliable misery. Roger went on with his sermon, but admittedly I stopped listening as closely to Roger and sat there thinking about the story.

I had had just the opposite response to *Groundhog Day*. Phil Connors awakes to the same unpromising day morning after morning—a strange hotel room, an annoying alarm clock, a meaningless job, a beautiful coworker who found him unbearable, all set in a simple, unsophisticated piece of America. In frustration, he tries to stop his miserable fate by a series of completely successful suicide attempts, only to wake the next morning—alive—to the same annoying alarm clock in the same pedestrian hotel room. Recognizing the trap, he misbehaves knowing it will have no consequence—he can rob an armored truck and the "next" morning nothing will be amiss. He bumps his way through the day with the same resentment and frustration the congregant had expressed. He punches, and the world punches back. And each day was just as miserable as the cold rainy morning had suggested. It might have taken Phil Connors some time to recognize it, but finally he does start thinking about the fact that he was stuck in this impossible world and that his punching the same way is having the same unwanted effect every time. If he was stuck here, he finally concludes, he might as well make it a little more bearable. So he helps an elderly woman and he makes friends with the town clown and he learns French and how to play the piano. And he wins the girl with whom he had so grossly and awkwardly flirted in the first of his Groundhog Days. He got to do the same day over and over, each day a little better than the last.

The people around him changed, his world changed, but only when he did the hard work of changing or accepting this new reality. But when he did change, their change, their acceptance or warmth or love, made his next improvement not just easier but more likely. But it had to start with him.

I met a lovely, earnest man named Mark Gorman recently. Mark is a metastatic melanoma survivor, and he told me that he carries with him in his wallet a fortune he unwrapped from a fortune cookie some time before: *You cannot change the wind, but you can adjust the sails.* That's what Phil Connor was doing, adjusting his sails, and when he did it, his boat moved in a new direction.

Groundhog Day is not a story of defeat. How wonderful, really, to live with the opportunity to get right today the mistakes I made yesterday. I can learn from my mistakes (and I will always make mistakes) and try to do better on the next try. I do not have to accept the reality handed to me; I can play a part in changing that reality. Well, within limits. So I keep trying, as Phil Connors did in *Groundhog Day,* to outmaneuver nature, to choose a different reality, or a different angle on the reality I cannot avoid.

My sister Nancy did this, in a smaller way, when she was five years old.

When I was seven years old, my brother was six and my sister was five. We lived in a white apartment building across from the station chapel on the Naval Air Station Jacksonville. My parents were Sunday school teachers, and each Sunday the five of us would walk across the street together. Before we left the apartment, my parents would give us each our allowance for the week. In those days, all the stores were closed on Sunday, so I suppose they were enforcing at least a one-day savings habit. Our allowance and the offering we got for the plate at Sunday school were each a dime. Before concluding that my parents were stingy, you should know that it was 1956, and in those days a dime would buy you a comic book or two candy bars. *Family Circle* magazine had a proud emblem on each cover: *Always 15¢*. It was a different time. (It was a time I think about fondly, when little girls dressed in crinoline, and nothing, even the price of a magazine, was supposed to change.)

This particular bright Sunday as we walked to the chapel, my sister took her two dimes in her cupped hands and shook them as we walked, listening to them jingle. But as she stepped from the street to the curb, one of the dimes popped out of her cupped hands, rolled along the sidewalk and down the curb, across a drain grate, and down into the drain. Without a second's hesitation, my five-year-old sister exclaimed, "There goes the Lord's dime."

She was certain that the dime remaining in her hands was hers. And perhaps it was not too unfair to assume that God had a better chance than she of retrieving the dime at the bottom of the drain. But what she was really doing was creating a reality she wanted. In my case, the reality I wanted was unachievable. So I struggle sometimes to see the silver that I still have left in my hands. Maybe, as so many say, the silver is an appreciation of our own mortality and therefore an increased appreciation of the days we have. It is worth living deliberately to get those days right, like in *Groundhog Day*.

This might be mindplay; it probably is, but what are the choices, really? I can live out my remaining days—however many there are—as a victim or I can try to experience them with an intensity that our mortality should have given us every day. I do not want to live as a victim. I even hesitate to write that my condition has worsened in fear that more people will look at me as a victim.

As I sat waiting for an appointment with yet another specialist at UNC Hospital a year ago, there was a woman in the waiting room with me, a woman who had just received a confirmation that she did, in fact, have breast cancer. She sat there, small and frail, a friend who had driven from Greensboro to be with her at her side, but a friend who would have to drive back that afternoon, and as she waited, her shoulders melted into shivering surrender. Tonight she would be alone with appointments to make, dinner to cook, and a job to go to in the morning. And she didn't look like she could even stand up on her own.

I had seen that look before, of course, in hairless women who were navigating the hallways at Georgetown, where I got my first chemotherapy—a hospital, like many, that seems to be in a perpetual state of renovation. Confounded by the absence of a once-familiar hallway, she had a look that admitted defeat. Beaten by cancer and by "progress."

Now, I don't think you can will your way to good health. To say that is to suggest that those who died didn't have will enough, that this cancer spread in me because I let it, and I know that is not true. But I do believe that none of us knows how many days we have, and it is a shame that any of our spirits capitulate to this disease—or any other—for even a day of the ones we have left.

But I have to acknowledge that one thing is clear: Every decision I make is colored by the fact that I know only that I will die before I thought I might, that each day has a number I cannot yet read. So when I decided to continue working in John's campaign after my rediagnosis, I was holding on to the life I wanted, even if the life I had was clearly less than what I wanted it to be. I adjusted my sails, but as little as possible.

There is a personal dignity that comes with

resisting the word "victim" and all that it means. Resisting by living each day and doing it well, even if, like Phil Connors, some of those days are still imperfect. I see it in the faces of women everywhere, some strong and healthy, some pale and hairless, who have a power in them. Was Donna in Minneapolis this determined before the cancer? Would Sharon in Atlanta have approached me before we had this bond? Not only had their spirits not capitulated, they had risen as they took each day into their own hands, made each day all it might be. Like Phil Connors, and like me, they probably hadn't done it the first day, but we all learned that how we adjusted made a difference in the life we had left.

There is just so much I can do to fight the disease in me. I know that. It frustrates me, it makes me afraid. I want control over it, and I have no hope of that. So I treat it as an asymmetrical war: I attack from another flank. I spend my time fighting for the health of women who have my disease but do not have the benefits of the great health care I get. I fight for more research to cure cancer.

I was in Cleveland to give a speech shortly after my rediagnosis in March of 2007. It was a lovely large room at the Cleveland City Club, the kind of stately room we don't build anymore in a magnificent old downtown building. After the luncheon speech some of the audience, which was mostly women, lined up to meet me or to have me sign a book or the program. There was a woman who had had breast cancer and her lovely daughter, a political supporter of my husband's, a scarved woman in the middle of chemotherapy. The thought of one woman in particular has stayed with me. She was wearing an ivory suit and stockings, so I assumed that she was working downtown. (I always assume that someone wearing stockings is working; why else would they wear them?) She leaned over and whispered in my ear.

"My name is Sheila," she said, "and I am afraid for my children. I have a lump in my breast, but I cannot get it checked. I have no insurance."

"Stay right here," I said. I called to Jennifer Palmieri, who was traveling with me, and we tried, right then, to get her connected with someone who could get her the help she needed, but by the time we found someone, Sheila had left. I assumed that her lunch hour was over and that she had gone back to work. At one level, this is a depressing story: a working woman with children who cannot get the health care she needs in a country of such abundance. But at another level, hers is a story of hope: She believed that we live in a country where things can change if we just whisper in the right person's ear.

She whispered in my ear. I am not the right person who can change things. But I am not the wrong person, either. It is like my sister's dime. She could want the dime for herself partly because she was five, but also because she couldn't understand that her dime in the offering plate was going to join other dimes and buy dinner for a hungry family or a jacket for a cold child. I certainly could have felt the same impotence in speaking out against a health care system that denied that working mother the care she needed that I feel fighting against the disease within me. And by thinking of myself as a single voice, I would give myself a perfectly reasonable excuse to do nothing. Or I could choose to see what I do as a small part of a collective effort that might change things. I remember protesting the war in Vietnam. Certainly my individual voice meant nothing, but the power was in the chorus of voices that might in time contribute to the end of that war. And I was in a war now.

Sheila gave me a great gift when she whispered in my ear. She reminded me that whether I had cancer or not, whether I lived five years or fifteen, my voice might be part of a chorus that could make a difference. I spoke about health care before meeting Sheila, but after she spoke to me, I recommitted myself to fixing a system that does not work for too many of us. I was luckier than I can say to have the opportunity to speak out. I am not the most talented of speakers, I don't know nearly as much as the experts know, but I have somehow found myself at a place where notoriety and disease open doors for me, hand me a microphone. I don't look away from any opportunity now. And with each short straw I draw, like the latest diagnosis, I recommit myself again. I may not have enough time for all I hope to do, but I do not have to accept my impotence against this disease.

Of course, every pain, every bump is a reminder of who will ultimately win the war, even if I win all the battles before that day. My job now is to stay alive until the doctors and researchers out there working find a cure. Using the days I have left as well as I can, hanging on to each day, another Groundhog

Day, hoping that one day those doctors and scientists will get it right and I will have enough time to get it right myself.

Until then, I live with cancer, adjust my sails, and remain inspired by the power of Sheila's whisper. I choose life.

CHAPTER 8

2008

The house was crowded this Christmas with family and school friends. Someone moved the Christmas CDs, apparently a well-intentioned attempt to clean up, but they chose as their first target the pile of Christmas CDs we had pulled out to play while trimming the tree. No one confesses, but even if they had, it would be no use; we can no longer get to the cabinet where the CD player is housed. My sister Nancy has come for Christmas, as she usually does, and has brought with her a dozen lovely framed pieces of art she has created. Displaying them in our family room away from the couches and the children, she chooses the protected location in front of the cabinet, but in front the cabinet that holds the CD player and the radio receiver. Christmas music seems out of reach today, the one day we really want it, while we decorate the Christmas tree. Modern life to the rescue: There is now Christmas music on a cable television music station. So we turn the televisions to the appropriate music channel, grab our baskets, and fill them with the ornaments I have unwrapped and piled high on the kitchen table. And singing along to the Christmas songs that really are Christmas songs (I don't use the word "Xmas," but some of the songs seem more like generic-brand unfamiliar Xmas songs than Christmas songs and we do not sing to those), we decorate the tree. Cate is home from school, her last school vacation before she enters the work world without three weeks off at Christmas. Two of her friends, Marlo and Chris, are passing through and spending the night before heading north. Cate, Nancy, Marlo, Chris, and I are trimming the big tree, and Emma Claire and Jack have corralled their father into helping them decorate the tree in the playroom. And my mother sits in a chair by the tree in the living room. In photographs it would look like the picture of a happy family, with the imperfections—like the Xmas songs—unable to be heard. And there were imperfections.

My mother lives in an assisted-living center near me, but she is at my house for the tree trimming, although I don't know that she even knows that. Now frail and sunken into herself, physically and mentally, she sits in the chair nearest the tree, periodically sleeping. When she awakens, she invariably points out something that disturbs her. An ornament she thinks is out of place, a person she doesn't recognize. My mother was once one of the most ferociously intelligent women I knew, and later that intelligence was a mask for many years of a departing mental acuity. Now no mask is opaque enough to hide the truth: The woman who was once my mother, like the six-year-old boy who was once my son, is gone, replaced by another person I love, but—in the case of my mother—one I do not always recognize and who does not always recognize me.

One by one, we each go over to her and tell her something about what is happening. Do you see the plastic stars over some of the lights, I asked. You and Dad helped put those on last year. With respect to my mother's contribution last year, this would be a generous description; with respect to my father's, an outright lie. Dad had almost no fine motor skills left in December of 2007. And this is the first Christmas since he died. She doesn't argue; she simply mumbles something unintelligible. I touch her hand and return to the tree.

My mother has never recovered from my father's death. He gave her great joy and great pain when he was alive, but now all she feels is the pain of his absence. So tremendous is the pain of the thought that he has died that sometimes she just rejects that truth: Sometimes she decides that he is simply somewhere else, maybe lost; maybe by choice because he doesn't want to be with her, a thought that breaks my heart; maybe he is just on his way here. Has Vince gotten here yet, she will ask. The experts say to let it go, and most of my family does that. When my sister tried to remind her of Dad's peaceful death, of his lovely funeral in Annapolis, of his interment across Weems Creek from the United States Naval Academy parade ground on which we used to live—in sight of our old house, in fact— Mother just got angry: *Have it your way,* she snapped. Nancy doesn't argue with her anymore. If Mother needs to believe that Dad is alive, is on his way, had lunch with her yesterday, Nancy lets her go where her mind seems most at peace.

I have never been as easy to get along with as Nancy. And I have an advantage, if the death of a child can ever be so described, because I can talk to my mother in a way no one else really can. When

Mother insists that Dad is still alive, that he was with her last night or that she doesn't know why he doesn't want to be with her anymore, I disagree with her. I know, I tell her, how easy it would be to think that he isn't really dead. I have been there, and I know what you are feeling, but in the end, Mother, all our wishing doesn't change anything. And from me, she takes it, she doesn't snap back. Somewhere inside her she understands that we have lost Wade, and she doesn't argue with me.

So when I have been talking to my mother and she looks sad, I sometimes think it is because with me she knows she cannot act in the play where my father is somewhere off stage. With me, he is dead. So as she watched me decorate, I thought that she looked sad because she knew I wouldn't play along with the willing suspension of belief. I sat my basket beside her and kneeled on the floor.

"Mother, you seem sad."

"I am." She didn't look over at me. Her eyes have become so deep set that they are little puddles with pencil drawings of eyes reflected deep in the bottom of them. She was looking somewhere past the tree, out the window and past the meadow behind the house.

"What is making you sad?" Imprudently maybe, I opened the door, but I was surprised to find what was behind it.

"It started thirty or forty years ago." Forty years ago, I thought. I started to calculate my own age. I would have been nineteen or twenty-nine. Nothing happened then that would have made her sad. What could it have been? And then I figured she hadn't any way of choosing thirty or forty years over choosing fifty or sixty.

"What was it?" I asked.

She fingered the corners of her mouth, speaking while she contorted her lips. I hope I understood her, for maybe it was one of the last lucid things she might ever say. Or maybe I hope I didn't understand her because it was hard to think these were her last clear thoughts. "I learned my hopes for how my life was going to turn out were not going to be."

I waited a few moments. She didn't say any more. "What does that mean, Mother?"

"The trust was supposed to be deep," she said. "The smiles were supposed to last forever."

We are not so different from one another. The hopes we have may have different backdrops, different accents, different details, but the central outlines are pretty much the same. The trust is supposed to be deep. The smiles are supposed to last forever. Did she figure out at forty-five that it wasn't going to be that way? Or did it dawn on her at eighty-five that life had fallen short? Or maybe it wasn't life in general, maybe it was one of us, one of the people on whose trustworthiness she had relied, one whose smiles were supposed to keep her company, who had let her down.

I hadn't understood much of what my mother had said in the previous six months, but this I understood. I am sad because my life has not worked out as I had hoped. It is no secret that my husband of thirty years told me that he had not been faithful to me. This is not about his indiscretion. He has his own battle to rediscover himself and realign his life. This is about my looking around me one day and finding, first, an ugly crack in the foundation of my life, and then finding out in time that the crack was deeper than I had first thought. Sometimes I need to say to myself what I said to my mother that night: "I want you to close your eyes, and I want you to spread your arms out and fall back into the pillow of all the people who have loved you."

In 2006, I was busy. I wrote a book and built

a house; rather, I actually wrote the book and I watched the house being built. I cared for two youngsters and measured for draperies. I sat with my husband as he planned to run again for the Democratic nomination for president, and I got treatments for the cancer that was in remission and periodic scans to make sure it was. I cleaned the rental house in which we lived so the landlords could try to sell it, and I negotiated with contractors to repair our longtime family home in Raleigh that had been flooded the previous Thanksgiving, forcing us to the rental house. I volunteered to find the names of children missing from the yearbook at Frank Porter Graham Elementary School and helped with the Book Fair. Cate and I went to Massachusetts to find a place for her to live in Cambridge when she started that fall at the law school at Harvard. And the two of us drove her furniture up when school started. I gave speeches and promoted my book, and I helped move my elderly parents from Florida to Chapel Hill where I lived when the assisted-living center in which they lived there told them they would have to go. I was busy. Too busy, it turns out, to notice that my life had left its orbit. My husband had an affair.

If you have picked up this book in hopes that in it there will be details of a scandal, you should now put the book down. This is my story, and my story is filled with pain and anger, with great erasures of my history and new outlines for my future, but it is not filled with the clatter you seek. The story from my side is quite a different story from the one of grocery store papers, a story played out too many times but rarely as publicly as my own.

It would be comforting to think I had sense enough to recognize that something was happening, but life had changed so often since Wade had died. There almost seemed no normal. For a woman raised in a military family moving all the time, a constantly changing life was not a sign of anything except normality.

John was gone a lot in 2003 and 2004 running for office, and although I saw him all the time in 2005 when I was getting treatment for breast cancer, I knew I would see him less in 2006. I even participated in his being gone. I thought he should do a spring-break trip for college students in New Orleans to help with the Hurricane Katrina cleanup. I agreed that he should work with various groups to help raise the minimum wage. His antipoverty work would take him across the country, and I knew that. When he told me that the political action committee was going to have behind-the-scenes videos made of some of these efforts, it didn't seem like that bad an idea, and it certainly didn't occur to me to ask about who was making them. It didn't occur to me that at a fancy hotel in New York, where he sat with a potential donor to his antipoverty work, he would be targeted by a woman who would confirm that the man at the table was John Edwards and then would wait for him outside the hotel hours later when he returned from a dinner, wait with the come-on line "You are so hot" and an idea that she should travel with him and make videos. And if you had asked me to wager that house we were building on whether my husband of then twenty-eight years would have responded to a come-on line like that, I would have said no.

I said as much in a speech I gave in April in Boston. What, one questioner asked after the speech, was the secret of a good marriage? I told her the truth: I don't know. We don't do date nights, we don't take long romantic vacations together. We care about the same things, but I think the real secret is to marry the right man. I thought I had. I was deeply in love with my husband for many of the reasons I talked about in the campaign. He was generous and cared about the plight of others; he was soft where a man should be soft and tough where a man should be tough. I could laugh with his staff about his weaknesses, teasing him, and he would good-naturedly laugh along. This was simply a weakness I did not expect.

John told me of his indiscretion on December 30, 2006, after returning from a tour to announce that he was running for president. My family had come for Christmas, and the plan was that he would announce in a series of cities and return to Chapel Hill for a final rally with his hometown supporters and his family. While he was gone, we talked—as we had our whole marriage—many times a day. We had talked about the initial announcement when he was in New Orleans—should he wear the green shirt or the navy? The navy. Was what he planned to say strong? It was. How were the children? The usual/unusual banter of a long-married couple with this odd twist in their lives. Again each day and again each night as he announced in New Hampshire and Iowa and Nevada, we talked, and finally, near the end of the month, he announced his candidacy at a rally in Chapel Hill, this time with his family by his side. After the rally, we came home to the chaos of a house full of family—my brother and his family and my sister and hers.

Before the announcement tour he had asked my brother to come with him to film it, since Jay taught film at the graduate film school at NYU, but when Jay found out another videographer was coming whether he came or not, Jay said no and had come here instead. Now the announcement tour was over and we were sitting in our family room, John telling us about the response in the various cities. John pulled Jay aside and asked him again to film the campaign or help him find someone to accompany him and film the campaign itself. The female videographer who had been on the announcement tour was not going to travel with him again. John did not tell him why, but Jay said he would. The next morning he told me why, or told me a version of why. He had made a terrible decision and had been with the woman. After I cried and screamed, I went to the bathroom and threw up.

And the next day John and I spoke. He wasn't coy, but it turned out he wasn't forthright either. A single night and since then remorse, was what he said. There were other opportunities, he admitted, but on only one night had he violated his vows to me. Some time after he got out of the race for the nomination, he admitted to more than that, but at first and for a year, it was a single time. So much has happened that it is sometimes hard for me to gather my feelings from that moment. I felt that the ground underneath me had been pulled away. I wanted him to drop out of the race, protect our family from this woman, from his act. It would only raise questions, he said, he had just gotten in the race; the most pointed questions would come if he dropped out days after he had gotten in the race. And I knew that was right, but I was afraid of her. And now he knows I was right to be afraid, that once he had made this dreadful mistake, he should not have run. But just then he was doing, I believe, what I was trying to do: hold on to our lives despite this awful error in judgment. Wade's death, the cancer, this indiscretion, each time our lives changed and each time we resisted the change, tried to make ourselves believe that our lives could go on and if we pressed hard enough, this new awful reality would not control our story. After everything we had been through we should have known, but knowing it on some intellectual level and actually doing it are two quite different things. We pressed ahead.

In 1972, my father was stationed with NATO in Naples. Driving in Naples is a challenge, or it was in the early 1970s. When the lanes headed south around the Bay of Naples were jammed, the frustrated drivers would simply take over one of the northbound lanes. The park at the bottom of the Posillipo where we lived was never a good place to walk, because the wide sidewalks could accommodate tiny Fiat Cinquecentos eager for a shortcut. At the intersection known as Crazy Corners, a stoplight was immaterial. The way to cross the broad intersection was to look straight ahead and press the gas pedal. Out of the corner of your eye, you could see an approaching, challenging vehicle, but as long as that driver could not be sure that you saw him, you could move ahead. He was looking at you, not the other way around, so you had the upper hand. And that is what I did on December 30. I drove ahead.

My husband, I suppose like every person in this position, had assumed that I would never find out, that the life he had built and cherished would not be at risk by an indiscretion. I spoke one time later to a media executive who said it was unlikely I knew everything. He was in a position to say that because he had stood once where my husband had stood. But, again I assume like most in this position, my husband did not want to risk the life he had built even after it was discovered, so he told me as little as he thought he could, as little as he must, with the hope that I would not leave him. I am certain he wished what he said were all true. I am sure, after all these months, he wishes that it had not even been one night, that when she said "You are so hot," he had turned and run. And I believe that he doesn't really understand why he did not.

And I suppose like most wives—or husbands—in my position, I wanted to believe his involvement with this woman had been as little as possible. A single night, another opportunity, but that was it and he had wanted away from her. He reminded me that he had begged my brother to come on the announcement tour. Jay reminded me, too. Jay, like I, had loved this man for over three decades. I spoke to him, Jay said. He asked me to come because he did not want her around him, but that she had insisted that she was coming even if Jay came; she was not letting go. Working behind the scenes, a friend of hers in the campaign made sure she was on the trip. Jay convinced me that John had no choice; she was going to come. He was as afraid, I suppose, as I was.

I hung on to whatever I could. I was, in nearly every sense, Tecmessa or the wife of any soldier or warrior who comes back from a campaign changed: I wanted my old life back with the man I knew and loved. I looked at his face and heard his voice, and it seemed possible, didn't it, that nothing had really changed. The man I married couldn't have done this. No matter how much I wanted it to be otherwise, like those women, I had to accept that the man who had come home to me was different and that our story would be different because of that. But knowing that and letting go of my expectations were two quite different things.

I spent months learning to live with a single incidence of infidelity. And I would like to say that a single incidence is easy to overcome, but it is not. I am who I am. I am imperfect in a million ways, but I always thought I was the kind of woman, the kind of wife to whom a husband would be faithful. I had asked for fidelity, begged for it, really, when we married. I never need flowers or jewelry, I don't care about vacations or a nice car. But I need you to be faithful. Leave me, if you must, but be faithful to me if you are with me.

It wasn't a premonition. I was talking about my own history. I had read my mother's journals, found them buried beneath a mattress in a guest room—I have no idea what provoked me, at thirteen, to look under a mattress and no idea why I felt compelled to read them, all of them, but I did. Notebook after notebook, getting to know a mother who seemed before that time to be in total control of her life. And reading, I discovered that my mother believed my father had been unfaithful to her when I was a baby. I will say clearly that I do not know if that is true. I only know what she suspected. She was serially pregnant in the late 1940s and early 1950s: My brother was born thirteen months after I was, my sister was born twelve months later. And my mother believed, rightly or wrongly, that my father had found other companionship while she was buried in babies. She even thought she knew where—the Willard Hotel in Washington—the place I had my senior prom, which must have been a bitter pill for her, although I had a suitably terrible time because, unbeknownst to her, I knew what that hotel meant to her.

My mother was beautiful. She had high cheekbones and brown hair that was red where it caught the light. When she met her first husband, who died in World War II shortly after their marriage, she had been horseback riding. Her hair was in braids. She wore jodhpurs, boots, and a white cotton blouse, the sweat from the Texas heat forming in the V-neck of the blouse. He was completely taken. My father saw her first when she was in layers of organza at a wedding rehearsal dinner. She had long legs, which are still shapely at eighty-five. She had the narrowest of waists and what was delicately called an ample breast. But she was more than that. She was witty and brilliant and competitive about everything except my father. When it came to my father, she was always on his side. In a series of houses to which we moved as a Navy family, she made each a home, decorating in a way that looks odd now in photographs but that I remember being the height of style then. She won flower-arranging contests, made knockout meals, edited the base newsletter, taught Sunday school, played golf, and started a charity antique thrift shop. She was the perfect wife of a naval officer. There was hardly a thing—except sing—that she couldn't do as well as or better than most around her. My father was blessed to have won her. And yet she believed that he may have cheated on her.

What believing that did to my mother I will never forget. I read about it perhaps a dozen years after it happened and it was still as raw, maybe even more so, as when she wrote of it. It undid the beautiful face and the ferocious intelligence; it mocked the family dinners and the charity work. She could be replaced in the most intimate of her relations by a face, likely a face not as pretty as her own, by a physique also not likely to have matched my mother's. She believed that whatever gifts of charm or generosity or intelligence she brought to their marriage, it had not been enough to compensate for baby diapers and dishes to wash. Someone without those responsibilities could laugh and fawn. And could take her place. As a Navy wife, she gave up all that she might be—which for her was considerable—to be with my father, to travel where he was assigned, to live where he was quartered, to raise their children to reflect well on him.

My father is of Italian descent, and it was family lore that he had a hot Latin temper. And there were plenty of screaming arguments as we grew up. But looking back I wonder that she didn't bait him, didn't needle him, accuse him in her soft southern accent until he did explode. She needed to be mad at him for something. The something she really needed to be mad about—a possible tryst at the Willard— was always unsaid, so the arguments were always about something else. Or the anger would turn onto one of us. We didn't understand it. Nothing seemed consequential enough for the level of anger. So we blamed a glass—or two—of Ballantine or a barmaid who had flirted with Dad or even a lieutenant who had flirted with my mother. It was all interior, all behind the walls of our quarters, never where it could be noticed or reported. We didn't talk about it to anyone; we didn't even talk about it to each other. To the rest of the world we were still the happy Anania family.

Mother kept looking for where she had fallen short. And the looking took its toll. She would swing from it being a failure of hers—she wasn't pretty enough; she wasn't as carefree as he; his mother never accepted her because she was a widowed Protestant, not a virgin Catholic, when they married; a hundred things it clearly was not—to its being a failure of his—how could he do this, he wasn't the man she thought he was, didn't his family mean anything to him, didn't his career matter. There was never a satisfactory place to settle, so she lived all those decades still loving him, but with something deep inside her that would always be restless, even after he died. "The trust was supposed to be deep. The smiles were supposed to last forever." Don't ever put me in that position, I begged John when we were newlyweds. Leave me, if you must, but do not be unfaithful.

My father, innocent or guilty, did what he could to make her feel that she was and would always be the center of his world. My father finally died in March of 2008, and for his funeral I gathered photographs of him to hand out, to decorate the reception. I am the repository for our family's pictures, and I can assure you there are at least ten thousand, likely much more. I went through each one. It was hard to find pictures of my father, for he, like I, was the photographer of his family. What I did find, though, was thousands of pictures of my mother, of the camera loving my sleeping mother or my mother reading the paper, or my mother looking wistfully from a train window or moving a treasured tansu she had found in a Japanese antiques shop. What I found was my father loving my mother. She had surgery to remove cysts from her chin. It is recorded with the kind of love necessary for scars. She is in the middle of cooking Thanksgiving dinner, a kerchief on her head, an apron halfway around her, a spoon stirring some large pot of unidentifiable delight. He adored her. He sang silly songs for her, wrote poems on the greeting cards, left notes on the refrigerator to his beloved Liz, or Diz. Whether that helped the self-loathing I don't know. Whether he ever really betrayed her, or whether he told her if he had, I don't know. But I saw them grow old together. And I saw him die and leave her here alone. For all the pain his real or imagined imperfections had caused her, she is to this day and will be until she dies unable to accept that she has to live a day without him.

When my pain hit, it hit me hard. It threw me to the floor in a way I thought, after the death of Wade, impossible. And the death of Wade made it even more difficult for me. I had said so many times that I cannot count them that after Wade's death I did not want John to have a single moment of un-happiness. And when Wade died, John had been beside me. We had felt the same things, needed the same things, leaned into each other in the deepest of ways. Every argument we had ever had evaporated in the face of this overwhelming sense of our—it seems strange now to say—oneness. For about six months we were never even able to be out of each other's presence, so essential were we to each other. When he had an appendectomy the summer after Wade died, Bonnie and Dan McLamb came to the hospital to sit with me, for I had not been without him since April. When he came out of surgery, I slept beside him in the hospital room.

I remember one day in the late summer of 1996 when he said to me that he did not want to go to the cemetery that day. "I know you need to go every day," he said, "and so I have gone with you, but I went not because I needed to go to Wade's grave. I need him, but I don't need to see his grave every day," he said. "I need to be with you." For months he had gone to the cemetery when it was hard for him to face that grave every day, and he had done it because he loved and needed me. What had happened between then and now? That man who gave me that gift could not be the man before me now.

How could this happen? What was I supposed to do? I had my mother's example of bitter acceptance, but what was I to do with that? Did she believe hers, like mine, was a single night? I found myself getting angry about other things, particularly in front of the children, just as my mother had done. And, with considerable self-loathing, I saw myself get short with them, too. Was I repeating my mother's story? She knew that if she left him, his career would suffer, as I knew. Was that why she stayed? I didn't think so, just as I didn't believe that John's career was why I stayed. We each had stayed because we loved the man we married. But was I destined to repeat a life of bitter acceptance? The possibility of my father's infidelity ate at Mother, I knew, but she stayed there, stayed with him and loved him, and after his stroke when he was nearly seventy she cared for him for nearly two decades with a selflessness that is almost unimaginable. Was that what I was supposed to do? And I was the one who would need the care. Although we did not know yet at the beginning of 2007 that the cancer had metastasized, we did know since 2005 that the cancer had spread at least to my lymph nodes, that there was some possibility of metastasis. I was the one who would need the selfless partner.

I often take respite in music, the old songs usually of the 1940s and of Broadway. I could listen to Dinah Washington or Lena Horne for hours. I compiled a book of lyrics so I could sit and sing the old songs, teach them to my children. But now they were hard; the love song I thought accompanied our marriage, accompanied our love affair, well, it hardly fit anymore. It had been Irving Berlin's "Always": *so lucky to be loving you*. I would walk around the house singing it and dozens of others like it. It was never John's taste, but it was the soundtrack that I wanted, that I chose for my life.

But now it was Stephen Sondheim's "No One Is Alone" to which I turned, hearing Mandy Patinkin's voice in my head. "Mother isn't here now. Who knows what she'd say. Nothing's quite so clear now." It was true, I knew. My mother had only shown me that staying and fighting for a marriage was possible—at a time when nothing seemed possible. I was bouncing from feeling sorry for myself— where I spent an embarrassing amount of time—to what might seem unachievable—feeling sorry for him. He was so clearly full of pain that what he had done had come to light. He was so full of pain and guilt and shame, it was hard not to want to reach out. And hard not to want him to reach back. Some gesture grand enough to wipe it all away. Some sweep of his arms that put us back together. A thousand photographs. Sondheim again in my head: "People make mistakes. Fathers, mothers, people make mistakes. . . . Everybody makes one another's terrible mistakes."

If it had been possible to view it all from some altitude, it might have seemed so easy to see how we came together and pushed each other away . . . for days, for weeks, for months. But I had no altitude at all. It was quite the opposite. I was too low to have any perspective at all. All I wanted was my life back. I didn't like this new life story; I wanted my old one. It felt so much like after Wade died—I wanted to turn back time so we could avoid the wind, avoid the woman, avoid the pain. Open a drawer and find my life again. But I would open a drawer and find my new reality instead. Everything I tried to do to allow me to go to some safe place turned out to be filled with the same pain. I would look at a happy family picture and break down. I tried to write and could not. Even now it is hard to put it into words.

When I die, my place in the lives of others will be filled by other people. I know this. It is true for all of us. Someone else will have your job; someone else will mow your lawn; someone else will kiss the cheeks of those you love. I worry about it, actually. One of the reasons that I spend time labeling baskets and organizing Christmas ornaments is that I have tried to create a world for my family that will last longer than the years I now have left. I am so in love with my family, so protective, that—odd as it may sound—long before I was sick, I would tell John whom he should marry should I suddenly die. Ann, then when Ann married, it was Kristen. Women I knew I could entrust with taking the same care I had taken. And now I was dying and he had chosen to spend time with someone so completely unlike me. It almost goes without saying, for I would never have, could not have, stood on a sidewalk in the hopes that some clumsy come-on line might work on a married man. But it wasn't just that; this woman was different from me in nearly every way. Not Ann, not Kristen, and not me.

It may not matter whether the hot glue goes

back in the glue basket or whether the snow globes are placed together on the shelf at Christmas or whether the birthday-present gift cards are in the same drawer, but if these inconsequential things might change, what of the things that have really mattered to me? At this moment I saw my death not simply as a transition for my family but as my complete erasure from my family's life and a complete erasure of the life I hoped they would have. I was afraid of what John might do when cancer finally wins, but he has been as assuring as I could have hoped. I am now at ease that John would not make the same choice in the daylight that he made in the dark, but for some time that thought dogged me, kept me awake at night, stoked my anger and my pain.

If this could happen, and it had, was I even someone with the ability to define a family or the outlines of a family's life? I must be less than that. I know what the books say: In an otherwise secure and loving marriage, such indiscretions have nothing to do with me. But I doubt there is a person to whom this has happened who did not, for some time, beat themselves with self-doubt and self-loathing. What did I do? How had I failed as a wife? Self-doubt wasn't that long a journey for me, frankly. The reason I was compulsive about learning whatever I needed to know on the campaign trail was that I was certain I would be humiliated if I was caught not knowing what everyone else in the room knew. So I learned four times the facts I would ever need, and I kept staff up nights finding answers to the questions I feared I might be asked. All the work to avoid being embarrassed was wasted; I now felt thoroughly and publicly humiliated.

Wade had written a short story when he was sixteen. Wade had gone on an Outward Bound Colorado climbing trip when he was fifteen, and he used his experience—he was, according to his own report, the least athletic and, according to others, the most thoughtful boy on the trip—for a short story he had to write the next year. "Summits" is about a boy on a mountain-climbing trip who is forced by circumstances to be a Good Samaritan first by carrying the gear of an injured camper and then by giving up the summit altogether. As he begins taking care of the injured boy the narrator confesses, "My only two thoughts were how bad I felt, and how hard it would be to pack two people's stuff and not hold the group up. (Truthfully, the only reason

I didn't want to hold the group up was so that I wouldn't be embarrassed.) This was exactly the situation I had been trying to avoid for the past two weeks (and, really, my whole life)." Wade had been trying to seem more athletic than he was in front of people he knew were watching him to see if he failed; I was trying to seem more self-confident, more appealing than I felt in front of my own larger audience. Like mother, like son.

And even before learning of a single night, I felt vulnerable to humiliation. Because of the fish-eye lens through which we all see someone in the news— the lens that makes some traits seem bigger and some seem smaller—people had too high an opinion of me, and I knew I had no chance of meeting their expectations. I have been described as self-effacing; that is true, but I should be described as "appropriately self-effacing." I, and I do so hope this is like most people, am certain I will be found out as not as smart or as generous or as thoughtful as I should be. And now this had happened. John knew. Perhaps this woman suspected. Was I to be found out like this? The possibility of public humiliation was a multiplier of my already numbing pain.

How to write on a few pages what that time

was like? Morning, afternoon, evening, sleepless night. Morning, afternoon, evening, sleepless night. Morning, afternoon, evening, sleepless night. It didn't seem to stop, and I could not see when it might. Just the opposite of James Joyce, I said no, no, no, please, no. So I did what I always do: I turned to others for support and love. I don't know what I would have done without my brother's voice. He let me cry when I needed to, and he made me laugh when I needed that. Another friend who had stood where I stood either honestly told me that my reactions were typical or generously lied that they were. I wasn't alone, but so much of the time I felt alone because I felt separated from the one person on whom I had so long relied.

I wanted to tell my sister Nancy, but I could not. Nancy had been married. She moved to Florida where they were going to retire to a home they bought together, and when she did, her former husband had brought another woman into their Ohio home. One of the things that has upset me is that I feel like my past is perhaps not what I thought it was and my future is certainly not what I dreamed. For Nancy, you could add to that that the actual pieces of her life were picked apart. Her clothes and jewelry from her Ohio home were put in garbage bags by this woman—some were missing when she finally retrieved them. Her furniture was rearranged, her children's rooms taken over by the other woman's children, her credit cards reissued to the intruder as if she were the wife. My life was figuratively injured; hers was literally dismantled. And Nancy, like Jay, loved John, loved how he had been so good to me, how he had cared for me through the cancer, loved what we represented: a marriage of equals built on love and respect. For the longest time, I could not take that away from her, could not compare my battle with her war. I could not tell her. I was wrong; when I did tell her, she was generous and honest. I needed both.

Nancy did not want her old life back, I did. I put on my earphones and dreamed. "Hard to see the light now. Just don't let it go. Things will work out right now. Ask me how I know." I thought I could fix it; I think John thought he could, too. But we were not living in our house, working on fixing it. We were separated. He was on the campaign trail. At first I could not, would not go. What would I say? I had said, in the months before, how this man had been my rock, and he had been, but I couldn't say that now. When I finally did campaign, I was pointed, so pointed I thought someone might suspect: We elect a vision and a person capable of making that vision become reality. If we yield to what we find appealing or engaging, if we yield to personality or appearance, we yield to an easy and false path. I could say that easily. It was, in fact, easier than I thought it would be. In a field of caution by the candidates, John had real vision. This is where we haven't been riven apart. We shared the honest discussion of our responsibility to our communities; we shared a passion for eliminating poverty and providing health care for those sitting outside the clinic doors. Whatever separated us, this did not. And I needed that, needed to feel that some part of my life with this man I had loved so long was intact. John had the most progressive policies and I could say that. I could do this, and in doing it, I could feel as if I were standing closer to the core of who he was and is than when I let his indiscretion capture my thoughts. I was with him in a sense. And in a sense, of course, I was not.

It turned out that a single time was not all it was. More than a year later, I learned that he had allowed someone else into our lives and had not, even when he knew better, made her leave us alone. I tried to get him to explain, but he did not know himself why he had allowed it to happen. In months of talking with him, I have come to understand his liaison with this woman, if I have, not as a substitute for me. It was more like his relationship with a former staff member. Most members of campaign staffs are young people who believe in the candidate or in his or her vision. There are a rare few who are obsessed with the candidate. A young campaign staffer in one state became fixated on me. He would make special arrangements for me and plan to be close to me when I was in his state; when he was fired, he continued to show up at town halls, staying in the same hotels I did. John had several like him, but one in particular whom I thought he let into our lives for much the same reason he had let in this woman. There is no reason to name the young man in the other state who followed me, and there is no reason to name John's obsessed fan. I will call him Jim.

Jim had first volunteered in the Senate campaign in 1998, working in fundraising. Julianna Smoot, who ran the finances, found him overbearing and did not want him even as a volunteer. What harm could he do, I remember saying then and regretting since. Jim volunteered for everything, making himself indispensable. He would drive John wherever he needed to go. Did John need something dry-cleaned overnight? Did he need his car washed? There was no job too menial for Jim. When you are busy campaigning, as John was, it seemed harmless, even helpful. When John went to the Senate, many of the campaign workers either went to Washington or stayed and ran the North Carolina office. Jim stayed in North Carolina, but he was openly jealous of everyone who went to Washington. He wanted to continue to drive John, and did when John came to North Carolina. Jim would drive across the state just to pick John up at the airport and deposit him at a meeting and then return him to the airport. When we were in North Carolina, he had his wife—who worked the night shift—leave McDonald's breakfasts for us outside our door before she went home. (I saw her one morning, and I told her to stop.) Could he help John's parents? How about his sister, what could he do for her? I now remember him telling me that my family didn't call on him often enough. A friend who worked in the North Carolina Senate office warned me about him: He is too possessive, he knows no limits, no boundaries. John was Jim's ticket, the friend said, and he was not going to let anyone get between him and John. That included me.

I complained about Jim. John had gotten used to Jim's unbridled loyalty, his willingness to do anything John wanted, and his obvious adoration of John. John and I would argue. Why are you so hard on Jim, he would say. I stood back for a while, but after Jim lied to us, I finally had the reason I needed to ban him from the house. It meant he could not drive John, that someone else would. He tried to find ways around it, to keep in contact, to keep as much of John's life as his own as he could. He bought cars like the ones we drove. He wanted to vacation where we vacationed. He had birthday parties for himself and invited all our friends. He sent daily e-mails to almost everyone we knew. And he became close with the videographer, who also did not understand boundaries. It was some time, but John finally saw what I saw.

In truth, the existence of a Jim made it easier to accept the existence of this woman. Those with any fame or notoriety or power attract people for good reasons and bad. Some want to contribute and some want to take something away for themselves. They flatter and entreat, and it is engaging, even addictive. I wanted to be less stern with the young fellow who followed me around than the staff thought necessary; to me he was simply sweet and wrongheaded, not dangerous. But too many are dangerous. They look at our lives, which from the outside in particular are pictures of joy and plenty, and they want it for themselves.

It took me some time to realize that I was lucky, really. I did not need to intrude into someone else's life to have happiness. Seeing these people as pursuing something they cannot or will not build for themselves, that they are unlikely to ever have, made me feel a little sorry for them. Their focus on achieving a style of life deprived them of any opportunity to achieve a purpose in life. They hurt me, and it still hurts, but whatever momentary pleasure they got, they didn't get what they wanted, and that must hurt, too. My life, at some level, is tragic. Theirs is worse; theirs is pathetic. I was still upset with John for allowing either of them into our lives, for being vulnerable to obsequiousness, for not kicking them out the door when they refused to leave. It makes it easier, too, that John is upset with himself in both cases for not doing just that. It has made it easier to forgive him that he cannot forgive himself.

That leaves, unfortunately, the long process of rebuilding trust. He violated a trust and then he lied. And even when he told the truth, he left most of the truth out. My mother's mother used to say that the intent to deceive is the same as a lie. We have spent much too long in that purgatory, so long it feels like hell. If he lied for a year and told another lie for another year, does that mean it takes two years to re-earn trust? It is not as easy or formulaic. Our life now is a mixture of living each day as a family, making dinners, packing school lunches, basketball games and Girl Scouts, chorus and Cub Scout sleep-overs. The stuff of real life, and here John has been all that it is possible to be. When I am sick or distracted, he is the caregiver I need, tender and attentive. John is not the photographer my father was, but these are his photographs, gifts of love. Like my mother unattractive in hair curlers, I lie in bed, circles under my eyes, my sparse hair sticking in too many directions, and he looks at me as if I am the most beautiful woman he has ever seen. It matters.

The harder part of the mixture is sorting out the truths and the diversions. Just as I don't want cancer to take over my life, I don't want this indiscretion, however long in duration, to take over my life either. But I need to deal with both; I need to find peace with both. It is hard for John, I can see, because it is something about which he is ashamed. But his willingness to open up is a statement that he trusts me, too. For quite a long time, I used whatever he admitted in the next argument and he was hesitant to say anything. That is, gratefully, behind us. There is still a great deal of sorting through to do—the lies went on for some time. And we both understand that there are no guarantees, but the road ahead looks clear enough, although from here it looks long. It helps that there are rest stops—building Legos with Jack, reading with Emma Claire, planning Cate's new house, hanging pictures of thirty years of memories—that remind us why we are together.

Forgiveness, I have been told, is the gift I give to him; trust he has to earn by himself. I am not going to suggest that that process is over. It is long from being over. I am still adjusting my sails to the new wind that has blown through my life. Nothing will be quite as I want it, but sometimes we eat the toast that is burned on one side anyway, don't we?

I also had the job of rebuilding myself. For so long I moved to a cadence set by someone else. While growing up, it had been my father's changes in duty stations. What was happening in my life really didn't, couldn't, matter. I moved for my senior year of high school, because that was his rotation schedule. When I married we both practiced law, but soon his career was on a rocket and he, not I, set the family cadence. It was fine with me. But now I needed a me. I needed the music in my head to be something for me. "Gray skies are going to clear up. Put on a happy face." The self-doubt that had fueled a need to overprepare had exploded with the recent revelations. I was overwhelmed and lost. There had to be places where I felt that I had value. The children might have seemed a natural place, but that was complicated—they were part of the family that I feared had not been enough. I gave speeches, but I was still afraid that people heard what they expected to hear. If they expected exceptional, they heard exceptional, even when I thought I was mediocre. I overprepared some more, writing new speeches for every group before whom I spoke. I still felt mediocre. Unlike when I was grieving Wade's death and could not eat, in this grief I ate too much, which was followed by immense disappointment in myself.

I wanted something that was mine. If I spoke publicly, I was asked about John. If I was asked to be on a board, it was because they had come to know me through John. I needed to be independent of him, maybe because he had been independent of me. Whatever the reason, I was on a search. And I found something that not only was mine but that I honestly wanted to do. I went to High Point one late-summer day with B. A. Farrell, my friend and the architect of our new home. We talked, as we did, of a thousand things, and he told me of buying a whole showroom of furniture at an enviable discount. He had doled it out to his various customers, but, he said, if you had a store, we could do so much more. By the time of the trip home, a plan was born: I would open a furniture store. I cannot say I had not thought about this before. I love the craftspeople and salespeople in High Point. I am guessing that it has something to do with creating a home, the function at which I am pretty sure I managed to succeed. I had talked about a store plenty, but always in the abstract. During the campaign it was just a dream, but now I was on a search for retail space in Chapel Hill. Hargrave McElroy's son Will helped me close on a small space; Lane Davis, who built our house in Chapel Hill, did the upfit, and I finally started buying furniture for my store.

I remember one time when John and I lived in Nashville, Tennessee. The living room and dining room were painted a pale green that was too close to a color that the military had used in every set of quarters in which I lived growing up. I wanted to paint, and we talked of it and talked of it, but it never seemed to happen. One day we bought a quart of paint and painted a big "X" on the living room wall. Now we would have to paint. That's what I was doing when Cate and I went to High Point one day and I bought a whole showroom of Italian furniture. There were nineteen mosaic tables; I would need a store in which to sell them.

In this world, I am not John's wife. My name is not in a tabloid. I am Elizabeth buying for a small store in Chapel Hill. John likes going with me to High Point, where everyone knows my name. He helped me buy a used truck. Vincent helps me move the furniture from High Point to storage to the store. Vincent is his own story of resilience. He worked for Lane, the contractor who built our house, and still does when Lane needs him. Vincent struggled with alcoholism and couldn't be counted on to show up when he was needed. About the time our house was finished, Vincent hit bottom, but he decided not to stay there. As I write, he has been clean for a year and a half, he has gotten his own apartment and a driver's license, and he is the most reliable, hardworking man I know. But more than that, he has great joy. He loves his life. The past is not what he wishes it was, but that does not mean he cannot create for himself the future he wants. Working with Vincent has been an inspiration to me, especially in the last months. And having a business that is just mine, that rises or falls on what I do or fail to do, makes me feel more like I have a place. So many people have said that I should advertise that it is my store, using my name and the celebrity or notoriety that my name carries. I don't argue, but I cannot do that. I am just Elizabeth buying for a small store in Chapel Hill. My husband helps me out there now and again.

CHAPTER 9

In the End

*I*n the end the way to view all that has happened is that I did my very best. I felt with every part of me. I loved with the whole of me. I ached in a way that reminded me that there had to be a corollary somewhere of incredible joy to balance the universe. And if I had loved less or doubted more or avoided the pains, I might not be assured as I am today that I have done in every circumstance what I would hope to do. Not every circumstance, surely. I have been angry beyond reason. I have been lost and unsure. But in every way I might have expected of myself, I have been true to that sense of what was true and right and clean. Maybe others had a better time, more intimacies, more skin pressed against skin, but this life is mine, these children are mine, this home is mine, and this imperfect man is like me. I am his and he is mine.

And in the end, what we want from life is too dear for words, for paper. Maybe that is why in every culture there is music that takes us places words cannot. So I sit here, the keyboard with letters in front of me, wondering how to say why I am able to breathe, why others I watch, whose breathing seems even more impossible, smile and laugh and live. And why I believe that I will smile and laugh and live. In the background I listen to Andrea Marcovicci sing "All the Things You Are." *You are the angel glow that lights a star. The dearest things I know are what you are. Someday my happy arms will hold you and someday I'll know that moment divine when all the things you are are mine.* And then the tempo steps up and wraps around me like a long chiffon scarf at the end of Andrea's long arms. What cannot be possible. Someday.

But there comes a point when the music ends. The trick is to have someplace to go when it does. Not to sink back into the hole in which the music found you, from where it lifted you. The trick is to go someplace that belongs to you, that was the perfect medicine for what you needed.

I measure my pains just as I measured my joys. When Wade died, I was lost, more lost than I have ever felt. Will Henderson and Matt Nowell had sat in our house after a Carolina basketball game a few weeks before Wade died. "Wade," one of them said, "in thirty years we can sit in your parents' seats at the games." "No way," I interjected, "when I am seventy-five Wade and I will be sitting there together." I did not just expect to raise him; I expected him to be my friend and companion every day of my life. He was supposed to enjoy all the pleasures of life, and I was supposed to be able to see him marry and have children. I won't see those things happen, but I did get to see Crystal from the Wade Edwards Learning Lab apply to college, I did get to see Elise put together a Web page for herself, I did get to see Philip grow into a fine young man, a fireman he told me.

When I got breast cancer, it was just another hurdle. It was high and I skinned myself time and again as I battled over it. But it wasn't as tough as Wade's death, so I could do it. Then the breast cancer spread to my bones, and after staying contained for more than a year, now it is growing again. I will do whatever the doctors tell me to do. I will take my medicines and get my chemotherapy infusions; I will avoid the foods I should not eat; and I will not do activities that could break my bones. Although I know that cancer now has the upper hand, it won't own me until it finally takes me. Until then, I will live as fully as I am able—absent horseback riding and skiing—and I will spend part of the time I have attacking cancer in a different way, by fighting for research dollars and an expansion of treatment to those like whispering Sheila who want to but cannot afford to fight the cancer in them.

We live not far from the country church in which John and I were married. I promised to love him for richer or poorer. We had nothing then. Really nothing, except debt from college loans. It is more than thirty-one years later, and we have more than we will need. I promised to love him in sickness and in health, and I have. And he has tended me in sickness; he has held me and fed me and taken care of me. I promised to love him for better or for worse. It has been, I have to admit, mostly for better. But there has been worse, and that worse has been tough on me. I turn sixty this year, and since I was fifty-seven, I have lived with that worse. But I choose to look forward, to the extent I am able, to make a place for myself and to make room for him to earn the trust he squandered.

A book of lists, the top ten, the worst scenarios. We seem bent on ranking all of our experiences. I have lost one child, but Gordon has lost two. I had Stage 2 cancer, but Sarah had Stage 4. I face whatever I must with a roof over my head and food on my table, and there are mothers and wives with nothing at all except my same griefs. The fact that I see someone surviving with a condition that sounds worse than my own or with fewer resources than I, well, it means I can survive, too, doesn't it? But what do I do with the lists in those moments when I don't feel like surviving, when the fight has left me? Have we failed, too, even at holding the short straw? I cannot even do this right? Gordon stands in the midst of the storm with his eyes so firmly on the horizon, and I cannot manage to lift my head.

When I looked at Gordon or Sarah, at any of those strong and miraculous survivors, I always looked for the tricks, the ways they managed to outwit the pain. They have to be there, don't they? It was hard to imagine, but I do accept that some people have looked at me the same way: What is the lesson that you know that I do not, the trick that I am somehow missing, the one that will take me through this experience?

I know now that I was always looking for the wrong thing. In the first place, Gordon and Sarah cannot have the answers for me. Just as I cannot have the answers for you. There are millions of tricks, as many tricks as there are fingerprints, each one belonging to just us. The answer wasn't in their lives; it was in mine. It is like going to the grave of a loved one: It is exactly right for some people and exactly wrong for others. In the second place, I kept looking for others to help me find the trick. God would make it right, would turn back time. The doctors would have the next medicine; maybe this one was a cure. John would say the right thing and make it all not so. Others could help me, so many have, but it was always in me—in me not just to find the answer but to make the changes I had the power to make.

Finally, it is not a book of lists, it is not a top ten. In a competitive world it is too easy to rank yourself against others. Gordon had to live through the deaths of his two sons; it is unimaginable. But the magnitude of his misery does not mean that I should have been able to handle more easily than I did the death of one son. The only contest we have is with ourselves. Wade wrote once, in an essay for a Latin exam, "The modern hero is a person who does something everyone thinks they could do if they were a little stronger, a little faster, a little smarter, or a little more generous. Heroes in ancient time were the link between man and perfect beings, gods. Heroes in modern times are the link between man as he is and man as he could be." That is our test. The man—or woman—we are and the man—or woman—we could be. I cannot be as resilient as Gordon Livingston or Rose Kennedy, both of whom buried too many of their children. I cannot be as strong and healthy as Lance Armstrong, who pushed his body over mountains after cancer. I cannot be as beautiful as Christie Brinkley, who faced her husband's indiscretions, too. I can only be what I am capable of being.

I have said before that I do not know what the most important lesson is that I will ever teach my children, Cate and Emma Claire and Jack. I do know that when they are older and telling their own children about their grandmother, they will be able to say that she stood in the storm, and when the wind did not blow her way—and it surely has not— she adjusted her sails.

The Next Chapter

When I began to write this afterword, I could type the words to make me feel as if I had finally landed in a safe port, that there was no further need to adjust the sails, that all the roughest seas—save dying itself—were behind me. I could even work to make the words be true. But when I confidently stepped away from my little ship and out onto dry land, I felt the earth give way beneath me. The place I had docked was so different from what I expected and wanted—a happy home with an adoring husband, a hard-won peace between us, where we could raise and nourish our youngest children, finally a moment away from a prying public. It was none of these. Had I landed in the right place at all? I needed, I suppose, to reboard my little ship, for there was more adjusting to do.

When Wade died, I did not want to try to find the me that existed before I was his mother. I wanted to stay his mother, to hold the boy who had cuddled with me on the couch, to listen to the secrets I was surprised a teenage boy would share with his mother, to do the little things that I had done for sixteen years. I could do them for Cate, and I could hold Cate, which were blessings, saving blessings in fact, but I did not want to stop being Wade's mother, too. I didn't have to reinvent myself; I was still a mother to Cate and to the memory of Wade. I had to reinvent the role, from mother of a living boy to mother of a dead boy—a sad transposition, but my task now was to make that role as comforting and satisfying as I could make it. Fourteen years after Wade died, I have grown to be at peace with that reinvented mother. His little brother, Jack, and I went to his grave on the anniversary of his death this year and planted flowers for the spring and summer—our statement that this boy still lives in his new form in our lives.

Now it was different. Though I had wanted to remain Wade's mother, if I reinvented the role, I knew I could no longer be John's wife. It was a sad and terrifying decision. I had been trying to reinvent the role of wife for the last two years—trying to find a place where I could be happy and still be

John's wife, despite his infidelity. Each day, it seemed, another little piece of my history chipped away. There was little comfort or satisfaction. There was no peace. And at the very end of 2009, I finally gave up trying.

It was just after Christmas, a Christmas that almost seemed as if we had found a way to live side by side, loving what we did of one another. My family came, save my brother and his family, and we did all the holiday things that warm me in some reliable but unexplainable way. The next generation—Cate and her boyfriend, Trevor; my nieces Laura and Jordan and their husbands, Lee and Kenny; and Cameron and Michael, the young married couple who live here with us, helping with the children and the furniture store I opened—were an affirmation that there is joy ahead. Watching my younger children and my grandnieces and grandnephew made Christmas magical as only children can. We had our usual gift exchange (each of us trading away the bejeweled belly dance scarf my sister Nancy contributed) and a silly sock exchange (each of us trading away the toed pair I contributed), and we ate and laughed and took turns riding the tractor through the woods. The roiling undercurrent that must have been there was buried in the joys of a boisterous family. And when they left, the silence must have exposed that undercurrent. The happiness that had filled this house did not fill this marriage. It was time to quit reinventing and making excuses. It was time to move on. Moving on is not really what I mean. This is the next chapter—literally and figuratively—but what am I supposed to do with the last chapter, with what I believed to be my story? We all want to at least know our life story—and with so many secrets kept from me I don't know that I will ever feel that I know what made up my own life story. There will always be a part of me that wants to know the story. But it was time to wrest control of that story from others and make my life my own.

Now I have to find the person that I was—or might have been—had I not fallen in love with John thirty-five years ago. . . . Thirty-five years. It was early 1975. He was sitting beside me in the lounge of the law school. He reached over to touch my shoulder, and he touched my breast instead. He flushed and stammered, and it took him even longer than it might have to get the nerve to ask me out. A kiss on my forehead at the end of that first date. This was a sweet young man. I could fall in love, and I did. Soon it was every day and every night. We would cash a check for $5.00 and go to Byrd's grocery store to buy corn, then to Cliff's Meat Market for a slice of ham to share for dinner. We hiked in the mountains near Boone, and we drove across the country to see the Grand Canyon, camping along the way. He would drive to the mountains of Maryland to spend New Year's Eve with my family, and he lived with my parents one summer when he worked in Washington, D.C. He—sometimes less than enthusiastically—played *$10,000 Pyramid* with me when it came on television as we were studying for the bar exam and—also reluctantly—agreed to pay for half of an Atari Pong game when it was on sale at Brendle's. We bought spaniels together and studied for law school together, and we talked and dreamed of a life together. We married in a country church not three minutes' drive from where I live today.

When I see John, I don't just see the today that others see. I see all these memories—the look on his face when he held our children as newborns, an embarrassed pride as he showed his parents through our first house, the loving way he looked at me when we were with others, the soft and vulnerable way he looked at me and held me when we were alone. We have raised four children, and we have buried one. So when I closed the door on the John of today, I also had to say good-bye to that sweet man whom I had loved for so long. It was not as easy as it might have seemed to anyone looking in from the outside, who knew only the John of today. And I have to wonder if he is sad, too, when he thinks of that young man.

So I have spent the last four months trying to accept the newest reality: I am consciously and willingly alone, with two young children who delight me and who test me, who make it easy to get up in the morning to see them and just as easy to fall asleep exhausted at the end of the day. I am the pieces of sixty years of life that once made a picture but no longer fit together, and I am trying to see what puzzle picture I can create from those pieces that remain. My delicious younger children; my precious Cate starting a life of her own in Washington; a house too filled with dreams and expectations ever to be a place in which I am totally at ease again; a small furniture store, the Red Window, that gives me pleasure and takes me out of the house, where—in the glare of a public that was told I was something quite different from what I am—I would sometimes retreat for days. I retreat not because I am uncomfortable with my decision. I retreat because the public glare distorted who I was and I cannot have it distort who I am now. There are press cameras at the end of my driveway and a mobile television unit set up outside my store. It is hard enough to find myself without that.

⁂

Much of what has happened in my life has unfortunately happened to many others. The difference was that I did it, for good or bad, with a spotlight shined on me—or, more accurately, shined on others and lighting me as a consequence. I had tried not to let the spotlight change me. Although it heightened my humiliations and therefore my reactions, I believed that I had recognized the distance between the me in the spotlight and the real me. My closest friends and I even made up a name for the woman in the spotlight: "Saint Elizabeth," who could do no wrong. We poked fun at that unrealistic image. The problem was then, and is now, that I had no control over the image. I never was Saint Elizabeth. I never pretended to be. I never was a monster. I certainly don't want to be. I was simply a person, increasingly fragile, who became more and more afraid of what tomorrow would tell me about my health, about my family, about my life. In many ways, I still am that person. But I was never as good, or as bad, as the shifting image portrayed. The most important thing to me is that those images and the weight of the public discussion of those images made it harder to sort out for myself who I was and what I wanted from the rest of my life.

This is where I want to make an admission. In writing the afterword for this book, I felt compelled to answer all the disproportionate descriptions of me, all the wholly concocted lies: What this person said was true, but these are the actual circumstances; what that person wrote was entirely a lie, no part of which is true; or what this other person said was a total fabrication made to excuse his own conduct. I wrote those pages and I sat with them, reread them (which was therapeutic), and then I deleted them. I do not know how I will feel tomorrow, but I know today that this is my life, and the more I respond even to the most ludicrous of the lies, the more I give my life over to people who are lazy or scoundrels or worse. I did choose, or by circumstances was forced, to sit down with these people in the past; why, however, should I sit down with them now?

We each want to write our own narrative. Now, more than anything, I need that. And I wish I could be good enough now that I do not care what fabricated image of Elizabeth is in the spotlight. But I admit: I am not that good. I care what people I do not know think of me. Do we all care? Or is it a weakness we acquire after feeling the warmth of the light? I think—and hope—we all care to some degree. I remember being a junior in high school and going over to the Chofu High School side of the field during halftime of a football game, when the cheerleaders of each team visited the other side of the field and gave a cheer for the opposing team. After the halftime was over, my father, watching from the sidelines in his dark green uniform, would leave for a tour of duty in Vietnam. I would finish the cheer for Chofu, then go hug my dad and watch him get into the driver's seat and pull away, not knowing whether I would ever see him again. Dreading the good-bye, I had cried during the whole cheer. I did not think about it while I cried. Only my father and the fear for him were inside me. Later, though, I wondered what those Chofu fans—whom I did not know then and have not met in the forty-four years since—thought of that crying cheerleader. What difference did it make? It made no difference at all to any part of my life, but I cared. And now that I am not sixteen, now that I am sixty with less time to right the image, I worry, too, that in the eyes of those who have replaced those Chofu fans— someone in Topeka or Elmira or Portland I have never met—I am that distortion. I want to yell: This is me, over here. To those who saw me briefly—in good moments or bad—I care what you think.

I never asked to be a public figure. When John ran for the Senate, I attended exactly three campaign events. But it happened and the warnings that you have no privacy did not scare me: What did I have to hide; foolish me thought then. I had lived my life on military bases with someone watching all the time. The door of my house in Raleigh was always open. The warning I did get was that my story could be public. The warning I did not get about being in the public eye is that anyone who wants to could write my story, and there will be some people who will believe it.

I laughed that I never was and don't want to be Saint Elizabeth. But I cried that I don't want to be seen—and maybe here I should admit, remembered—as the worst of the portraits of me. Is it too much to want your obituary, when written, to be about your own life, not the lives of the worst people who came into your life? About the lies they told for their own purposes? This is who I am—too concerned with what others think, too stubborn to give into the feeding frenzy, and too wrapped up in making a new life for myself and my children to think that anything else I do for the rest of my days matters remotely as much. I do my best to keep that last, which is in my heart, also in my mind, but, honestly, there is a roiling in me, piqued at each new frenzy, each new heartache, each new lie.

When John left the race for the Democratic nomination for president, I spoke to the staff assembled at the campaign headquarters. Lost in the story told by a few is the intense affection I felt for so many on the campaign staff. These mostly young people were my second family, like soccer teams and high school friends of my children had been before them. In fact, among them were some of those teammates and friends. I had known many for a decade, some for longer. I watched them find mates, I listened as they told me when the mating did not work, and when it did, I held their children. They were never inferiors to me. I felt, perhaps wrongly, that I could argue with them—we were all engaged in a single cause, one that mattered if we got it right. After John withdrew from the presidential race in early 2008, I spoke to them as we gathered for the last time. "The race is over for John, and in most ways it would seem that your efforts for his candidacy were for nothing, but that is not right. When someone mentions health care, remember that your work got out the first health care plan among these candidates and set the bar for what they would have to say. And pat yourself on the back when we get universal health care, because you did that. When the next president talks about poverty—and both these remaining candidates have pledged to address

it—pat yourself on the back. When we have mean-
ingful standards on emissions and climate change,
remember that you were there first, and pat yourself on the back." My eyes—and theirs—were filled
with tears. I loved these young people, and I wanted
them to know that they had done something important and worthwhile.

As I spoke in February 2008, I still did not know
that John had had more than a one-night stand, and
I do not think that most of those in the room or the
volunteers and supporters around the country believed that he had. (There is a sense, I am afraid,
that everyone on the staff knew what John was
doing. I do not believe that. I believe now that a few
knew and remained silent, even with me. Their odd,
sometimes belligerent, silence with me makes me
think so. I believe now that a few knew and were
actively supporting his misconduct. But it hurts me
to think that there is a stain for those young people
who simply believed in a cause and in a flawed
man.) We in that room knew one thing for sure:
John had policies and ideas in which we believed,
just as we believed in him. The lesson I hope they
carry is that there is no shame in believing and fighting for those beliefs. When what you lived for every

minute of every day for years collapses, it is impossible not to look for the flaws. But John had not lost the nomination to his indiscretion. He had lost the nomination to two extraordinary candidates. The truth about his conduct and the conduct of those who helped him conceal his lies unraveled later. Those young people were pure and good in their effort. Their time with him was not wasted.

And as I thought of them, a voice in my head kept repeating: Listen, Elizabeth. Listen to what you said. You believed in that man. Maybe you were seeing what you wanted to see, what you needed to be the truth. Believing in people is what we should do, and I still want to live by that. It would be lousy to live any other way, hard as that is to believe right now. Living and believing and loving is not a waste. Just as I was telling those young people that their time on a failed campaign had not been wasted, I needed to tell myself that my time in a failed marriage had not been wasted. I am still talking to myself about that.

It is not so easy. Have I really wasted thirty years? How many sad onetime lovers have asked this question? How can I now measure how well I spent my life? It was easy to see what remained—

above all else, my children. My precious Wade, lost to the winds across tobacco fields fourteen years ago but still with me every moment. Wade was as sweet and gentle as a boy could be in this callous world. We helped him be that. Nearly perfect Cate, inquisitive, funny, wildly intelligent, and not the least judgmental. We were there for her, too. Cate and I spoke on the phone the other day and I asked her if there was anything that I did that made her the adult she is today. "Everything," she said. But can you point to something? "It was everything, Mom. Your belief in us, your support, your love. You put us first." I was still dissatisfied—please e-mail me if you think of anything in particular—but we moved onto other pressing issues like did I know where a jacket that she left in my car eight months ago was. (Really.) A little while later I got an e-mail from her: "You went to look for my white jacket." That was her example, and it turns out she was right. I had hung up the phone, gotten up from my desk, and looked through her room and through all the closets in the house until I found the missing jacket, now boxed for mailing. It is the little things after all. I hope to give tender Emma Claire and charming Jack the same intangible gifts, a mother's time and love, and I hope that they grow as their older brother and sister did, that they are granted the strength to rescue themselves and their own relationships from the insensitive seas that now surround them. This is enough, a gracious plenty, as my mother would have said. And, yet, when I look around me, there is more. More that I missed when I was so preoccupied with finding a way to be a wife when I no longer believed I knew what that meant.

The blessings are there. Even when I holed up in my house for a while—which I did (those cameras at the end of the driveway can have that effect)—Cameron and Michael were inside. I don't know who loves Cameron and Michael more—the children or me. I only know that we can cry on one another's shoulders, that we can get angry at the same tabloid headline, that we cannot stop laughing when a preteen embarrassed at some scatological reference slips beneath the dinner table to hide, that things are more fun when they are there. Cameron and I went to High Point for the furniture market, held twice a year. We talked all the way there, walked and shopped for the store for hours, and then drove, mostly in silence, all the way home. We can talk more when our feet don't hurt so much. Cameron can let me bask in the affection I got there from strangers—a blessing too immense for words: manufacturers from Atlanta; salesmen from New Orleans; a retired guidance counselor from Chicago who had come with her husband; Ed from the parking lot, who gets mad when I pay for parking somewhere else when he would let me park for free. I could enjoy their affection and turn and see Cameron enjoying my getting it. It is the little things like that.

And this week, I talked to Steven and Sarah at the Wade Edwards Learning Lab and my mother, though I could not understand her much. I will talk about her in a few weeks when I am allotted twelve minutes on a forum on motherhood here in my hometown, and I met with the young man—a science teacher in his day job—who puts the forums together because he wants to keep storytelling alive. You have to like that. I called my dearest friend and the children's godfather, Glenn Bergenfield, and laughed with him, and I e-mailed friends about the UNC women upsetting Northwestern in lacrosse. I talked to my sister, as I now do almost every day;

she was here last week to see Mom and to help with the monthly sale at the warehouse for the Red Window. I made plans to have lunch with a friend. Softball and baseball games for the children are starting and maybe I can talk Bill Spiegel, whom I have known for forty years, into coming with Cameron and me to a game. I worked on an editorial on the influence of corporate money on the body politic. I talked to my doctors; I got radiation treatments on a place on my hip that was bothering me and I spoke to everyone in the waiting room—as I am wont to do every morning—and got hugs today from Sue and Jerome. And tomorrow morning while I wait, Phil Lister, my Internet friend whose daughter Liza died the year that Wade did, and I have plans to talk. I have all of that. Sometimes you have to write these blessings down, remind yourself what remains. Life did not grow barren just because I closed a very big door.

And I have something that those young people in the campaign gave me—a sense that all things are possible if you are willing to put yourself on the line. You cannot stand back and hope for the best. You have to act. I wrote in this book about seeing your situation for what it is and taking action, but I had not acted myself. Maybe it was that thirty-year investment, maybe it was that I could not separate the flawed man before me from the boy with whom I fell in love in 1975. It does not matter now. But finally at the end of 2009, I realized that I could not simply wish us to some halcyon final days. And I thought about what I needed to do. I thought of what I told those young people gathered in the campaign headquarters. I decided that I do not want to be that person hoping for a day that may never come—that sad, bitter, unhappy person. Finally I have taken the steps I need to take to never be that person. It is one of the things I left behind when I closed that door behind John.

❧

This Christmas was our last as a family. We did not know it, of course. In fact, it seemed in many ways in the months before as if the tender thread that bound us all together had strengthened. In time, however, that tender thread unraveled and sent me into a new and cold chasm after Christmas. The details are not important. To each of us who throws out our lives, their histories, it seems at the moment

that everything we say and do determines some out-
come, but in time it all fades. It wasn't that one
thing. It was simply the last thing. One day, I did
not want to try anymore. The harsh words that had
hurt me once did not hurt. I simply wanted to be
away from all of the things I had tried to accept. I
wanted to take a long shower and be away from the
lies my husband had told me and the woman he
told them about, and the awful couple who had
helped him live the lies, and even the now-dead
friend of his who had at some level made at least the
last of it possible. I wanted to be that girl who
walked into the law school in 1975 with such naive
and noble expectations.

I am just like you. I went through hard days,
and like so many who see hard times, sometimes I
was surprisingly resilient, and sometimes I collapsed
under the weight of it—*it* being Wade's death, by
far the worst of the *its* in my life, or breast cancer, or
a husband's confession of a one-night stand, or cancer again, this time with an unreadable time card
for my remaining life attached, or feeling that others were keeping secrets from me, or watching my
husband's dreams come to an end, or finding out

then what the secrets were, little by little until I learned, more than eighteen months later, as the world learned, that the one-night stand was in fact a relationship, and finding out months after that, that my husband had fathered a little girl. Those closest to me saw the torment inside me, saw it seep into other parts of my life. But now as I try to put that life back together, to find the new imperfect and, yes, unsaintly me, I need to think about myself and who I really am and what I really want. And like many women, what I want revolves around my family.

Jack is ten this year and Emma Claire is twelve. I want to send them to college. I want to be well enough to be the mother to them that I was to Wade and Cate as they grew. I want, as with my two older children, to have a house full of teenagers working on biology projects or making giant greeting cards to send to younger siblings at camp, or standing halfway out the front door during a UNC game because they concluded that the fate of the Tar Heels depended on where they were standing while they watched the game on television. I want the silly forgettable moments that made being their mother so rich. I want Christmases for them that have happy endings. I want to walk them to the door of the next part of their lives secure in the knowledge that they are deeply, unreservedly loved. I want to live to hold Cate's children. I can measure when Emma Claire and then Jack will graduate. Cate's children—if she chooses to have them—are an unknown. But I will assume that Jack will graduate high school in eight years, that Emma Claire will have chosen a college major by then and that Cate will have handed me at least one child to hold. Eight years. That's what I ask for. I will be sixty-eight years old. And if I get there, I know I will want to live longer, that I will ask for more—who wouldn't?—but right now I want to live for eight more years, to finish the one job I know I did better than any other. When it ends, as it will for all of us, there is always the fate of the Johnsons.

The Johnson family is buried not far from Wade at Oakwood Cemetery in Raleigh. Oliver and Gerald each died when they were two, about a year apart. Their brother Robert died as a young soldier in the first world war. The boys' parents lived for decades more, but now they are all dead, all buried, and all together. How much grief must have passed through that mother's life? And yet there she lies, beside her boys. In the end, there is peace. If we are strong, if we are resilient, if we are stubborn and filled with hope, if we know how to love, there is peace before that, too.

And, honestly, that is enough.